An Introduction to
CANADIAN
ARCHAEOLOGY

An Introduction to
CANADIAN
ARCHAEOLOGY

David L. Newlands
Royal Ontario Museum

David L. Newlands

Claus Breede
Royal Ontario Museum

Claus Breede

McGraw-Hill Ryerson Limited

Toronto Montreal New York London Sydney Johannesburg Mexico Panama Auckland
Düsseldorf Kuala Lumpur New Delhi São Paulo

An Introduction to Canadian Archaeology

1 2 3 4 5 6 7 8 9 0   THB   5 4 3 2 1   0 9 8 7 6

Printed and bound in Canada

Canadian Cataloguing in Publication Data
Newlands, David L., 1938-
    An introduction to Canadian archaeology

Bibliography: p.
Includes index.
ISBN 0-07-082339-1 pa.

1. Archaeology — Methodology. 2. Canada —
Antiquities. I. Breede, Claus, 1944-
II. Title.

CC77.H5N49   930'.1'028   C76-017098-3

CONTENTS

Preface

This book was written to provide an introduction to the basic techniques of historical archaeology in Canada. As educational institutions and local historical societies show more and more interest in this fascinating subject, a basic presentation of field and laboratory techniques becomes a necessity for would-be diggers.

Canada today is awakening to the importance of the past, and the unique contribution it can make to the understanding of our contemporary situation. The increase in the number of small historical museums and restoration projects is part of this developing interest in historical preservation and interpretation. More high schools are offering courses in local history, a trend that means a much more sympathetic public for the archaeologist in the future.

Recovery of information on the early European settlers of Canada, the object of historical archaeology, cannot and should not be left to the small number of "professional" archaeologists, skilled as they may be. There are just not enough professionals to deal with all the important areas of archaeological interest, let alone to direct all the field excavations that could and should be undertaken. The problem may be solved, partly

The careful removal of soil to reveal archaeological remains is only a part of the task of the field worker.

at least, by improving working relationships between the so-called amateur and the professional archaeologists, so that the available resources in skilled volunteer work and financial support are joined with the back-up facilities of museums, university research laboratories, and library reference collections. It has been the authors' experience during many seasons of field work in Ontario and New York State that when properly motivated, volunteer teams can work to professional standards. They are not paid to dig; their rewards are the satisfaction of a job well done and the refreshment of body and spirit that comes with sustained physical activity. Many volunteers bring to the site skills such as surveying, photography, drafting, or conservation, primarily employed outside of archaeological study

but valuable contributions to the dig. Unfortunately, such human resources are often overlooked when archaeological study is planned.

It is proverbial among archaeologists that no two professionals go about their field work in the same way. There are many systems for recording and preserving information from a dig. The techniques described here have been tested over a period of years in Canadian field work, and are the current product of an evolving approach to historical archaeology—an approach that attempts to maintain accuracy in recording and recovery of information, while retaining a high degree of adaptability to the diverse types of historical sites being dug at this time. These techniques are not meant to be either definitive or the ultimate, authoritative

The keeping of detailed and accurate records in the field ensures that information learned from excavation is available for further study in the research laboratory.

"method." To regard them as such is to minimize the potential for growth in historical archaeology and to risk failure in future response to situations not yet anticipated.

For many years archaeologists have used the metric system of measurement. The gradual conversion to the metric system in schools, industry and government in Canada has encouraged the authors to use this system almost exclusively. Tables for conversion from English to metric measurement are widely available and can be found in most bookstores.

The subject of underwater archaeology is not discussed in this text, underwater historical archaeology being so specialized. This is not meant to imply that the subject is unimportant. Quite the contrary: this aspect of archaeological investigation continues to expand in both Canada and the United States. There are a number of good basic texts such as George Bass, *Underwater Archaeology* (London: Thames & Hudson, 1966), that can be consulted for further information.

This book was made possible by the encouragement and practical support of our colleagues at the Royal Ontario Museum. The manuscript was read and criticized by Mr. Donald Webster, Curator, Canadiana Department; Mr. Francis Pryor, Assistant Curator, Office of the Chief Archaeologist; Dr. Edward J. Keall, Assistant Curator, West Asian Department. Their advice and interest in the text have helped to improve the presentation of archaeological techniques. Parts of the text have been read by Mrs. Elizabeth Phillimore, Senior Conservator, Conservation Department; Miss Janet Holmes, Curatorial Assistant, Canadiana Department; Mr. Leighton Warren, Head Photographer, and Dr. Howard Savage, Research Associate, Ornithology Department, and president of the Ontario Archaeological Society. Dr. Ronald Farquhar, of the Department of Physics, University of Toronto, helped to improve the section on resistivity surveying. Special appreciation is due to Mr. Gordon Thompson, of Bramalea, Ontario, who has given freely of his time in reading various drafts of the manuscript and has helped to improve the clarity and impact of the text.

The authors would also like to express their appreciation to Mr. W.B. Robertson for photographs taken in the offices and labs of the Museum.

All the people mentioned above have helped to improve this book, but the final contents and presentation are the responsibility of the authors.

This book is dedicated to Marion Newlands and Dagmar Breede, who have suffered the consequences of their respective husbands being too busy to do their share of the essential domestic tasks that are part of family life. We promise to make up for our neglect.

January 30, 1976
DAVID NEWLANDS
CLAUS BREEDE

CHAPTER 1

INTRODUCTION

The physical remains of Canada's past are being destroyed at an alarming rate. This is due partly to the rapid expansion of urban centres into areas that were formerly rural and the extensive re-development of many older parts of the urban landscape. The alteration of the landscape results from the pressures of an expanding population and growth in industrial activity. Rarely a day passes that the media do not report new housing schemes, industrial plants and highways for part of our living space, with only a minimum appraisal, if that, of the impact of these projects on our historical patrimony. Governments have been slow to respond to calls for studies of the archaeological impact of new housing or industrial expansion.

At the same time there is a growing awareness of the importance of the quality of life and the importance of our environment to the healthy functioning of an industrial society. There is more interest in studying, recording, and in some instances, preserving the evidences of our ancestors' settlements and industries. In an effort to keep ahead of the impending destruction of sites of historical significance, the archaeologist has become an important member of the organizations concentrating on the study of Canada's heritage. For example, it is not unusual to find the archaeologist and the restoration architect listed together as advisers in planning for the restoration of an historic building. Some consulting firms are now employing archaeologists to help in assessing the effect of proposed public works on historic sites.

The field of archaeology that specializes in the recovery of evidence of European settlement in Canada is generally known as "historical archaeology." This area of archaeological study centres around the period from the sixteenth, roughly, to the twentieth century. The term "colonial archaeology", when used to refer to historical sites in Canada, is misleading, since many important sites are post-Confederation (1867).

Historical archaeology in Canada differs from pre-historical archaeology in that the main emphasis of the former is on European influences. The distinction between pre-history and history is not a complete one, however, as contact forts and settlements where Native Peoples encountered European trade and culture are of interest to both groups of archaeologists.

Historical archaeology also includes, to varying degrees, the field of industrial archaeology. Industrial archaeology deals with the early form and development of industrial activity. In Europe, with its long history of industrial development, industrial history and processes and their impact on the emerging social environment have become a distinct research discipline. In Canada, however, two separate disciplines have not yet evolved. The difference between industrial archaeology and traditional forms of archaeology, where digging in the ground is a prominent research method, has caused some archaeologists to insist that the name industrial archaeology should be changed to "industrial recording" or "industrial history." The distinction between industrial and historical archaeology is one of range of interest rather than of technique, especially when one remembers that field surveying, recording, photography and historical research are common to both. The distinction becomes more academic when one considers that industrial

Plate 1.1. The remains of a late nineteenth century earthenware pottery kiln excavated at the Huron Pottery, Egmondville, Ontario, in 1973.

sites such as potteries, glassworks, etc., may require digging in the ground to complete the research programme.

The amount of digging at any site will depend on the nature and completeness of the historical evidence, as well as the information to be gained from excavation. For some sites a complete field survey with scaled drawings and photographs may suffice, whereas others may require extensive excavation. In evaluating a given site the historical archaeologist's first task is to assemble all the documentary evidence associated with the site and its broader regional context. Sources of information may include land-title records, early maps, atlases, census reports, fire insurance records, contemporary business directories, local newspapers, and early photographs—to name only a few. The documentary evidence may reveal that historical scope of the site is important enough to warrant further field work.

The field survey will provide information on the nature of the remains at a site, the attitude of the present landowner to excavations, and the

facilities available for any proposed digging. The decision to conduct field excavations will then depend upon the evaluation of the combined results of the historical documentation and field survey.

The historical archaeologist should keep in mind that his work may interest many specialists in related studies: art historians, museum curators, restoration architects, social historians, anthropologists, industrial historians, and those interested in the decorative and industrial arts of the past. Restoration architects may want to know the location and method of construction of various buildings, while a museum curator may be interested in the ceramics and glassware used in a particular house. Industrial historians concerned with the development of the pottery industry will want to learn about kiln construction techniques. Social historians may be interested in data detailing the social practices of a particular area. Local historical societies may want materials for display and reference.

The ultimate value of the archaeologist's work

Plate 1.2. *Artifacts uncovered in the field are analyzed in the research laboratory as part of the process of interpretation of the results of an excavation.*

will depend on the questions he asks about a site and the thoroughness of the methods he employs to find the answers. The range of questions that might be asked of a single site exceeds the competence of most individual field archaeologists, and specialists from other sciences are often called in for advice and further studies. The trend in archaeological research is to develop a research group or consortium to plan and oversee the work so as to provide data for each discipline taking part. Ideally, evaluation of an iron foundry may involve an industrial historian, a metallurgist who knows smelting processes, a draftsman, an architectural engineer, and a field archaeologist. The results of such a team effort are likely to be far more significant than anything one person can produce. The pattern of team research in historical archaeology is the same as in other branches of the subject, in which complete interpretation and direction of field work involves more than the description of artifacts, soil layers and architectural features.

The completion of a field excavation does not end the archaeologist's work. The evidence uncovered in the field will have to be studied and then reported, in diagrams, maps, photographs, and written text. Publishing the results of an excavation is as important as the dig itself; information unavailable to anyone but the excavator reduces field work to a sophisticated form of treasure-hunting. In the Province of Ontario, the recent legislation governing archaeology requires that all licensees file a preliminary report on results of each excavation and a statement of plans to complete their publication.

Historical archaeology has grown markedly in the 1960s. In 1967 there emerged two scholarly organizations devoted to the study of our more recent history. In England, the Society for Post-Medieval Archaeology publishes newsletters and a journal and convenes regional conferences on topics of archaeological interest. In America the Society for Historical Archaeology publishes a newsletter and journal devoted to historical sites in North America.

CHAPTER 2

THE SCOPE OF HISTORICAL ARCHAEOLOGY

To the beginner the extent of historical archaeology as a subject must seem overwhelming. First there is the time span involved, and then the multi-cultural aspect of the settlement of Canada: as well as French and English Canadian sites, other European influences are manifest throughout the history of the country. Finally, the archaeologist is faced with the diversity of types of sites: domestic, industrial and military. A typical military site could be a French or British fort, or a Hudson's Bay Company fort, the latter a commercial as well as a military centre. At some forts there were continuous dealings with the Native People and such places, known as *contact sites*, exhibit both Indian artifacts and European trade goods. The historical archaeologist is well advised to choose a specialty before he begins his work, and to learn as much as possible from both the historical evidence available in libraries, museums, and archives, and the published reports of those who have done similar work in the past.

Domestic structures range from the settler's one-room log cabin to the French Canadian manor and the Ontario homestead. Houses may have stone or brick foundations, piers, or posts to support the wooden sills of the building above. The archaeological evidence for such structures may be as extensive as a continuous wall foundation, or as scanty and elusive as a post hole. The style and scale of construction will reveal the social and cultural background of the designers and original inhabitants. The historical archaeologist must also be knowledgeable about the history of Canadian architecture and the variety of out-buildings to

be examined and explained: kitchens, smokehouses, ice-houses, root cellars, and the ubiquitous privy.

In the industrial category are foundries, furniture and textile mills, potteries, glassworks, breweries and distilleries, brick yards, quarries, lime kilns, and industrial housing estates, that bridge the gap between domestic and industrial sites.

Within the limits of a single chapter or a small book, it is impossible to deal with the evidence from all the sites excavated in Canada in the past decades. Instead, a number of sites will be discussed, to indicate what evidence the trowel may uncover and the kind of information that may assist the archaeologist to understand it.

Domestic Sites

Investigation of domestic sites frequently centres on the more unusual houses of the day, partly because of the distinctive features of the structures and the events associated with them. Not everyone in Quebec lived in a manor house, nor did all people in Ontario have homes in the style of the twelve-room house at Cherry Hill, Peel County, Ontario. The study of these unusual buildings however, does provide a standard by which we may measure the living conditions of poorer people.

In digging at domestic sites the most common objectives are: (1) to retrieve information on structures and artifacts before the destruction of the site; (2) to provide a collection of period ar-

Plate 2.1. Excavations at Ile des Soeurs (Nun's Island), an island in the St. Lawrence east of downtown Montreal.

Plate 2.2. The remains of the manor house of Jacques LeBer, Senneville, Quebec.

tifacts that will help in dating other sites; (3) to retrieve specific information for restoration purposes, and to augment documentary sources. A few examples of typical Canadian domestic sites will show how these objectives can be reached.

The Jacques LeBer house on Ile des Soeurs (Nun's Island), in the St. Lawrence off Montreal, was a late seventeenth-century French Canadian manor house, built by a family prominent in the French fur trade. The Royal Ontario Museum excavated the site in the summer of 1969. Little if any excavation of early French Canadian manor houses had been done, and a threat of destruction to the site made it urgent to dig the remains for a representative collection of artifacts.

At a manor house in Senneville, Quebec, also built by the LeBer family, in the early years of the eighteenth century, the owner initiated excavations. In some places the walls of the house still stood several metres above ground level. A garden setting had helped to make the ruins pleasant for visitors, but the prospect of continued deterioration of the walls encouraged the R.O.M. to study the substructures. A raid by

Benedict Arnold that destroyed the house in 1776, provided a terminal date for all the artifacts found in the earth and associated with the building.

The threat of destruction also figured in the examination of Cherry Hill, the homestead of Joseph Silverthorne, in Peel County, Ontario. Excavations were begun in 1972 to salvage information on the site's structures and associated artifacts before the construction of a new highway interchange. The fact that the original building would be moved to a new location to be restored as a museum encouraged the archaeologists to retrieve any remaining evidence of the early life of this particular homestead. The artifacts, after study and restoration, would be a guide to the interior furnishings of the house, indicating the kinds of dishes, cutlery, and general household goods, the inhabitants used.

A fourth example of an excavation at a domestic site is the short-term dig at the Fryfogel Inn, near Shakespeare, Ontario. This building, a former Canada Company stage coach inn of the mid-nineteenth century, was to be restored by the Perth County Historical Society. Archaeological exploration was undertaken in 1974 to discover as much as possible about the furnishings of the building during the time it was used as an inn. Future excavations may also show the location of early wells, or the remains of early out-buildings, such as smoke or ice houses, that might be associated with an inn.

The study of domestic sites has its problems. Most troublesome is the fact that owners rarely preserved records of the changes to a structure or the land around it. Additions such as driveways, trenches for sewers, water and gas lines, and numerous other conveniences are typically made during the life of a structure. As the life of the pioneers changed so did the structures on the land. A farm's smoke house, ice house, and dairy would be demolished. The barn, because of its continued usefulness, became one of the most durable homestead structures.

The most common architectural features remaining on a domestic site are foundations. These are usually of wood, brick or stone, and may be shallow or deeply set. When the foundation of a structure is located it is then possible to relate the artifacts around it to the history of that particular foundation. If artifacts are found in the foundation trench, they were deposited in the soil used by the builder. Artifacts found around the foundation will tell of the building's uses, while artifacts found in layers covering the walls will indicate when the building was destroyed or abandoned. The artifacts associated with a foundation will usually provide a range of dates for each stage in the life of the structure, enabling the archaeologist to determine an overall date for the structure, and to compare it with the dates of other artefacts on the site.

Excavation of a domestic site is rarely dull, as each has its problems and unique features. With the Jacques LeBer house, the problem was to locate the remains of the buildings under blasting rubble from a nearby bridge construction and accumulated silt from the St. Lawrence River. This house, built between 1665 and 1670, was still visible in 1958 when its owners, the Congregation de Notre Dame, sold the island for a housing scheme. The approximate location of the site was determined by studying aerial photographs taken before the bridge was built, and plotting the location of the ruins onto a recent topographic map. Discussions with the various contractors involved in dumping the land-fill helped to estimate the depth of fill that had to be removed before the original land surface would be visible. Removing soil with a bulldozer is risky as it may destroy some of the evidence, but removing the compacted rubble by a more cautious method would have used up all the time available for excavation. The original land surface was reached after some 2 feet of overlay had been removed with heavy equipment. Careful digging through the next 6 inches of soil exposed the manor's foundations. Stone foundation walls 75 centimetres thick, the remains of which stood about 35 centimetres above the original floor of the house, were eventually uncovered.

The excavation of a series of surveyed squares revealed the size and design of the original house (see Plate 2.3). It was 7.4 by 15.4 metres in size, and the remains of a fireplace with an adjacent bake oven were uncovered at the north end of the house. To protect the house from Indian attacks two poorly constructed bastions were added in 1693, one on the northwest and one on

Plate 2.3. Aerial photograph of excavations on Ile des Soeurs showing walls of the buildings. Baulks have been removed from some squares to delineate walls more clearly.

the southeast. The foundations of a stone bakery, and tenant farmer's quarters, measuring 6.2 by 10.7 metres were also uncovered.

At the Senneville site, located at the western end of Montreal Island on the banks of the Ottawa River, the landscaping made it impossible to excavate the site in a regular pattern of squares. In place of a regular pattern, trenches and small squares were positioned to avoid the landscaping and to expose other structures at the site. The trenches had to be shored up to prevent stone debris falling on the diggers. The manor at Senneville originally had four bastions, each two storeys high, and a walled courtyard, which had enclosed a three-storey stone house.

The Cherry Hill homestead presented different problems. The main house was built in 1822 and occupied by descendants of the original settler until 1910. The excavation of the grounds, sponsored by the Ontario Archaeological Society, was continually hampered, both by treasure hunters and by a shortage of time and funds. Treasure hunters continued to destroy the work of the archaeologists even after a watchman had been employed. (Vandalism on a site is a problem that even the most ardent archaeologist often cannot solve.) Digging uncovered a stone house 7.7 by 6.2 metres, believed to have been a dairy or smoke house, and a smaller stone structure, 1.6 by 2.8 metres at its uppermost point, a basin-like feature with a perpendicular-sided ditch. The basin and ditch were mortared, presumably to prevent the loss of water. They are believed to be the remains of a water-collecting system.

Artifacts recovered from domestic sites are the facts upon which descriptions of a material culture are based. The two Quebec sites produced quantities of green and brown-glazed earthenware pottery, nails, kitchen utensils, cabinet hinges, glass trade beads, fragments of faïence and delft pottery, musket balls, bottle glass, pins, pewter buttons, English Queensware dishes, clay pipes, and many other objects. The excavations provided an important reference collection for comparison with artifacts from other sites in Quebec. The diversity of artifacts from Cherry Hill was greater than that of the French sites, and included imported English porcelain, earthenwares, and hundreds of different household and personal objects, spanning the one hundred and fifty years of habitation at the site.

Industrial Sites

Pottery and glass artifacts are among those most frequently found at historical sites; identifying them and establishing a source and date of manufacture helps in the study of similar artifacts from other sites. Such industrial remains may also interest students of the decorative arts and collectors of Canadiana.

Plate 2.4. Part of a stove after cleaning shows the decorative art from a home in nineteenth century Ontario.

Plate 2.5. A contemporary photograph of the Ahrens Pottery, Paris, Ontario, taken in the late nineteenth century. Photo courtesy Brant County Museum, Brantford

Potteries

In nineteenth century Canada potteries produced various vessels for use in the pioneer home and marketplace. The potter capitalized on a local supply of clay, a source of running water, abundant forests of hardwood for use in firing the kiln, and the market provided by nearby population centres.

In 1851-52 the census of Upper and Lower Canada reported twelve potteries. The number of works continued to increase until the 1880s, when the census reported ninety-two in the two provinces. Then a rapid decline in the number of potteries began, due in part to the competition from products made of glass and metal, lighter, more durable, and cheaper. By 1910 fewer than twelve earthenware potteries were operating in Canada; the last of them closed in the 1920s. In eighty years, the potter and his business flourished, then passed away virtually unnoticed. Crocks disappeared from kitchen shelves and cellars, to be replaced by the more attractive new alternatives. Because many potteries were located in or near towns, their workshops and kilns were converted to other uses or taken down to make room for succeeding trades. Business records such as bills of sale,

ledgers, trade photographs, and catalogues also disappeared. The most lasting reminder of many potteries is the many sherds, or fragments of pots, that littered their sites. Regardless of the changing uses of the land, the ubiquitous sherd withstood the builder's machines and the farmer's plow. Sherds can still be found at the Davis Pottery, Toronto, now the site of a bank building, at the New Hamburg Pottery, Waterloo County, Ontario, now partially covered by an apartment building, or at the Christian Hess pottery in the town of Zurich, Ontario, now under a lawn.

Reviving interest in this early Canadian industry has animated the search for evidence of it, and students of the fine arts, local history, and the history of technology and other forms of archaeology are seeking information about early potteries and their products. In some cases the objective is to identify the makers of pottery now in private and museum collections, a difficult task because most potters did not mark their wares. In some cases the vessels' characteristics may reveal the tradition their maker worked in, if not his identity.

In addition to earthenware potteries there were a small number of manufacturers of stoneware pottery, such as the Brantford

Stoneware Manufacturing Company, of Brantford, Ontario, and Hart Bros. and Lazier, of Picton and Belleville, Ontario. These factories produced more durable types of pottery, but the clay had to be imported from the U.S. Stoneware potteries suffered the same fate as the earthenware potteries, and disappeared about the same time.

An earthenware pottery operation included at least four different stages. These were: the cleaning of the clay in a *pug mill;* making the pots; air-drying of the *green* pots; and firing of the pots in a kiln.

The clay for making pottery was dug and hauled to the works by horse and wagon. The clay was then dumped into a pug mill where it was worked by a series of rotating knives mounted on an upright wooden shaft. The shaft was turned by a horse. The addition of water and working of the clay removed any stones and produced a thick fine mixture. The clay was permitted to dry slightly, then cut into blocks and stored in the pottery building. In winter the clay might be stored in the cellar to prevent it from freezing.

In the pottery room each pot was formed, or *thrown,* on a foot-operated potter's wheel. It is reported that a skilled potter could produce forty to fifty small pots an hour. In some cases the potter also produced moulded wares, and decorated pots with applied designs of grapes, raspberries, lion heads, etc. One of twenty-two pottery moulds recovered from a mid-nineteenth century Ontario earthenware pottery site is shown in plate 2.6.

When the potter had thrown a pot, it was dried in the sun, or in a drying room where heat from a cast-iron stove would dry the green pots slowly. When a quantity of pots had accumulated, the potter would stack them in the kiln. Small pieces of *kiln furniture,* such as wedges, stilts, or saggars, to name a few forms, were used to keep the pots from touching one another. After the kiln was loaded, the door was secured and a fire started in the kiln fire-mouth. This first firing, a very difficult process, took several days and produced what was known as *biscuit* ware.

After the first firing, the pots to be glazed were dipped in a liquid made of silica (or white sand),

Plate 2.6. Pottery mold and decorated cover.

Plate 2.7. The rectangular kiln of the David Burns Pottery, Holmesville, Ontario.

red lead, and a binding substance such as gum arabic. The pots would be allowed to dry and then heated in the kiln a second time until the glaze fused to a glassy surface. Glazing made the pots waterproof, and improved the surface colour.

The pottery kiln was typically round in shape, as found at the Eby Pottery, Conestogo, Ontario, and the Huron Pottery, Egmondville, Ontario, or rectangular as at the David Burns Pottery, Holmesville, Ontario (plate 2.7). The kiln would have a *beehive* or *bottle*-shaped top. In the beehive shaped kiln the heat of the fire either passed up over the pots and out through vents in the top of the kiln (an up-draft kiln) or up over the pots and then down to the base of a chimney at the bottom of the kiln (a down-draft kiln). All bottle-shaped kilns were of the up-draft type.

There was no way to control the amount of heat in a kiln; the potter had to regulate the firing temperature by the addition of small amounts of fuel. Here training and experience were crucial. The potter had to know the characteristics of his clay and the effect of wind and fuel on kiln temperature. It was not unusual for a part of each kiln-load to be discarded, as some pots would be blackened by smoke or direct contact with flames, or warped by the intense heat in one part of the kiln. After a firing, the kiln temperature would have to be lowered gradually to prevent cold air from entering and cracking the pots. Any damaged wares were usually dumped in a nearby ravine or beside the pottery building itself. Accumulations of such pottery form what the archaeologist calls *waster dumps*.

No pottery kilns are known to have survived intact, but there may be sufficient evidence in the brickwork of the base and footings to indicate the arrangement of the interior. Any pottery should produce waster dumps containing sherds indicating the full range of pot shapes produced, and of problems the potter met in firing his kiln. Quite frequently an examination of the sherds will show glaze colours not usually attributed to the particular pottery in question. Potters' tools and other equipment may also be recovered.

Glass Factories

In Canada's early years, glass was imported from the United States, Great Britain, and France for use in windows and household containers. Canadians continued to rely on imported glass throughout much of the nineteenth century, as low import duties and limited demands made any large investment in local glass factories very risky. The earliest documented Ontario glass factory, the Mallory Glass Works in Mallorytown, was established in 1839, but like many of the earliest Canadian glass businesses, its life was short—it operated for only one season. A contemporary newspaper story suggests the factory's demise was "owing to the unreliableness of the foreman. . . ." The Mallory Glass Works produced containers (bottles, flasks, bowls and pitchers).

The story of the Napanee Glass Factory, of Napanee, Ontario, and the excavations there in 1968 illustrate both the difficulty of establishing a viable glass factory and the archaeological evidence that might be found at such a site.

The greatest demand was for window-glass. In 1881, John Herring, an industrialist who had settled in Napanee in 1843, established a factory to meet this demand. Beginning with a capital of somewhere between $40,000 and $50,000, he built a factory with a furnace, iron chimney, workmen's cottages and storage facilities. Prospects for success were apparently good, as Herring travelled to the United States to learn the latest manufacturing methods. The factory opened in the fall of 1881; by 1883 it had closed. Subsequent attempts to form a joint stock company to re-open it failed.

Apparently, the Napanee Glass Works failed through Herring's inexperience in glass-making, inability to compete with imported glass, employee problems, and the general effect of a depression in world trade in the early 1880s. Herring had to import glass-blowers from Germany, Belgium, France and England, and it was hard to keep these employees once they came to Canada and were offered higher wages elsewhere. The development of glassworkers' unions also led to conflict between Herring and his staff.

The limestone of the Napanee area is only lightly covered with soil and vegetation and several features, such as the main factory building, a circular masonry structure—probably the foundation of the flattening oven—and the outline of the building that enclosed the oven were all easily identified in aerial photographs.

After an initial survey the site was divided into 30 metre squares, and a surface collection was made within each square. The concentration of artifacts indicated the areas that should be investigated.

The main building was 25 by 20 metres and divided lengthwise into three units: the outer

Plate 2.8. Aerial photograph of the Napanee Glass site, Napanee, Ontario, showing building outlines (right of center), a spur railroad track, abandoned roadway (upper left), and modern road and railroad (right).

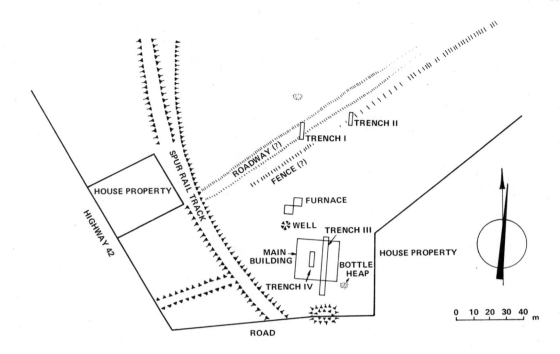

Figure 2.1. Plan of the same area as aerial photograph of plate 2.8.

two were of equal size, about 8 metres wide, and the central unit was 4 metres wide. The two outer rooms were each divided in turn into three small rooms. The central room was probably a corridor. Two short walls, each 4 metres long, formed the foundation for a porch along the south side of the building. The stratigraphic relationships and the purpose of the building were investigated by excavating two longitudinal trenches, which divided the width of the structure into three equal parts. The massive size of some of the interior walls seemed to corroborate a contemporary newspaper account of the works which states that the furnace was built on stone walls, 5 feet in thickness and in the centre of the main building.

In the glass-making process, silica (from sandstone), which had been crushed, washed, and dried, was mixed with alkalis and heated in ceramic pots until the mixture had become a liquid. Salt impurities, called *gall*, had to be skimmed off the melted glass before it could be used. Hollow blowing pipes were inserted through openings in the sides of the furnace and dipped into the pots. A *gather* of the melted glass

was removed from the furnace and blown into a long cylinder about 1.5 metres long and 0.25 to 0.30 metres in diameter. The ends were then broken off and the cylinder cut lengthwise with a diamond knife.

The flattening oven stood next to the main factory, in its own wooden building. The base of the flattening oven, which was all that remained of the original structure, had been constructed by mining out of the bedrock a circular hole about 9 metres wide and 0.4 metres deep. The sides of the hole were reinforced with a stone wall of carefully laid, roughly squared stones cemented with lime mortar. This wall varied from 0.4 to 0.9 metres in thickness. Three or four courses were laid against the sides of the hole from the bottom to the surface. The remains of two small buttresses were uncovered; these may have been part of the exterior vaulting used to strengthen the dome of the oven. The only evidence for the superstructure of the flattening oven was mortared bricks, indicating the general curvature of the dome. In the flattening oven, cylinders of glass were placed on a large horizontal iron wheel that revolved slowly, so that by the time

Plate 2.9. A selection of bottles from the artifacts found at the Napanee Glass Works, Napanee, Ontario.

the wheel had completed one revolution the cylinder had flattened and could be moved to the annealing oven. The flat sheets of glass were stacked on end and moved slowly through the oven towards the cooler end, opening into the cutting room. Here the glass was cut into smaller sizes and packed into wooden boxes for shipment.

Artifacts from the Napanee Glass Works were mostly fragments of window-glass, although a small dump of bottle fragments indicated that containers may also have been produced, if only in limited quantities.

Military Sites

More than any other historical site, the military fort recalls the bloody story of the defence of Canada and the struggle to establish our sovereignty over a vast territory. In response to interest in early forts, all levels of government in Canada have been active in restoring or reconstructing many of the more important ones. The historical archaeologist has been asked to help in the search for evidence of early structures and the artifacts associated with them, important information for the architect and historian planning the reconstruction of buildings vanished from the landscape. If there are questions on restoration, it is the task of the archaeologist to help verify the location and dimensions of original structures.

Military forts are a basic part of the pattern of settlement in Canada. In many places they were the first structures erected, the nuclei of permanent civilian settlement. There are some two hundred known forts in Canada, and many played a leading role in the history of the country. Forts were located on coastal areas (Citadel Hall, Halifax), on lakeshores (Fort York, Toronto; Fort Henry, Kingston), rivers (Fort Niagara; Lower Fort Garry), or on hills overlooking stretches of open land (Citadel of Quebec). Many of the early military forts became the centre of what later became provincial capitals, for example, Halifax, Quebec City, Toronto (York), Winnipeg (Upper Fort Gary), and Victoria, British Columbia.

Military forts could be either temporary or permanent establishments. Evidence for temporary forts is often difficult to recover, but the permanent fort is one of the most straightforward sites to dig. The size and arrangements of structures in a fort will vary with its size and location. There may be any number of different buildings, such as the powder magazine, blockhouse, soldiers' barracks, guard house, officers' quarters, privy, kitchen, to name a few of the more common. Fortifications varied from walls built of stone or brick sometimes with interior storage spaces, to simple earthworks and palisades.

Archaeological investigation today is frequently aimed at verifying details of the buildings, especially their exact location and dimensions, as many of the early plans and drawings were inaccurate or unclear in this regard. Luckily for the historical archaeologist there is a considerable amount of documentary evidence, since the military was generally efficient at reporting on the construction and maintenance of buildings.

The Royal Ontario Museum's excavations at Fort York, Toronto, in 1973-1975 were typical of digs at military sites. Fort York was begun in 1793 by John Graves Simcoe, the first Lieutenant-Governor of Ontario. Most of Simcoe's buildings were of green timbers; within about seven years they had deteriorated badly. In 1803 a residence for the Lieutenant-Governor was constructed on the site, and a number of new buildings went up to the east of the original garrison to replace the earlier ones, which had been demolished.

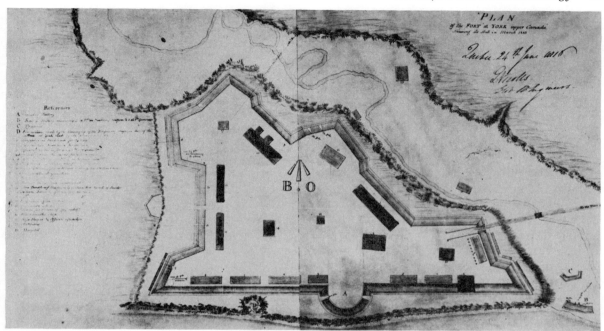

Plate 2.10. *An 1816 plan of Fort York shows the guard house immediately south of the entranceway. This guard house was the subject of archaeological excavation in 1974 and 1975. Courtesy Public Archives of Canada*

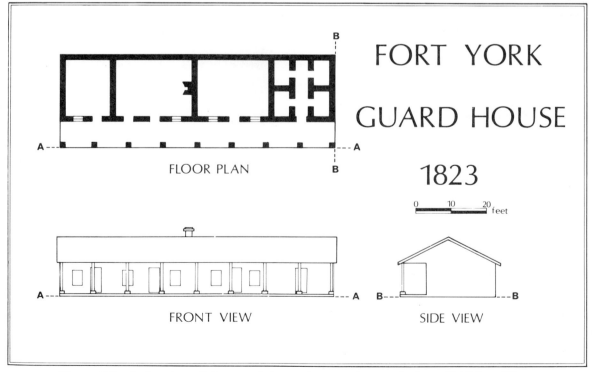

Figure 2.2. *A drawing of the guard house from a plan made by a British military architect.*

The garrison fell to the American troops in 1813 in spite of a number of last minute preparations. After the Americans had left the fort, the British defenders then began rebuilding and strengthening the garrison. By 1816, eighteen buildings stood within the walls, providing accommodation for up to a thousand officers and men (see Plate 2.10). With peace came prosperity and the size and strength of the garrison diminished after 1816.

The opportunity for archaeological investigations at the site of the original guard house, located just within the east gate, aroused considerable interest among those who felt that it should be reconstructed to provide additional office and storage space. The guard house, shown in Figure 2.2, contained quarters for the duty guard, the orderly room, and the cells or "black hole" for prisoners. It was a squared log building, measuring approximately 24 by 8 metres with a porch along the west wall supported by a number of pillars. An 1851 survey of the fort shows the guard house, but by 1871 a larger structure, approximately 32 by 18 metres, identified as a "hut for 2 NCO's and 45 men," appears in its place.

In the 1973 excavations fragments of the stone floor of the latter barracks building were uncovered. In 1974 the fragments of stone floor were removed to reveal a layer of brick and mortar debris. Artifacts among the debris included a great many fragments of clay pipes, military buttons, bottle glass, children's toys, early coins and trade tokens. Below the debris layer was a regular pattern of waterlogged wooden beams and planks. The regular pattern of these beams suggests that they are part of the remains of the earlier guard house structure. It will take many years to complete a thorough archaeological study of Fort York; its size, like that of many military forts, demands a number of successive digs to recover all the evidence underground.

This chapter has attempted to show the diversity of sites examined by historical archaeologists. It is hoped that the prospective field worker is encouraged thereby to undertake the research necessary to a fuller understanding of what may be expected at a site, and the specific problems to be solved before a successful dig is begun.

Chapter 3

THE USE OF DOCUMENTARY SOURCES

Before a spoonful of earth is turned, the historical archaeologist must make a thorough examination of the historical documents on the site or industrial process in question. Fortunately a great variety of written information is available, in local libraries, municipal, provincial or federal archives, and in private collections. Evaluation of documentary information about a site helps the field worker to formulate objectives for a dig, and to pose questions the digging may answer. If historical evidence conflicts, then field work may clarify the problem and help to resolve the differences. On the other hand, where ample and reliable information exists, there is little reason to excavate; time, money and human resources can be allocated to other sites awaiting study and exploration.

The extent of the historical research necessarily depends on the site and the purpose of the field work. With a large military installation of national importance, such as Fortress Louisbourg in Nova Scotia, a staff of researchers will be available to search far and wide for a possibly significant shred of information. These large sites are not common in Canada; most historical research is concerned with small local sites such as houses, inns, and industries. This chapter is intended as an introduction to the historical resources available for the study of these sites, whose archaeological interest does not depend on their size.

BEGINNING THE RESEARCH PROJECT

The place to begin historical research is in the communities near an interesting site. This is especially true for nineteenth century sites, where the local community may still have primary documentary records not yet available in archives.

The community library is the first place to go as it will probably have a selection of local histories, published or in manuscript, original photographs of people, buildings, and landscapes; early maps, county atlases, family geneaologies, early copies of local newspapers, and possibly even artifacts of importance. Most important of all, the library staff may have first-hand knowledge of local people who can supply further information, historical documents, or other significant materials. Quite frequently the local librarian will do some research work for you, if she has time. But be careful not to expect more research assistance than the librarian can provide. Remember also that she may have to limit the actual handling of fragile documents, if continual use would cause permanent damage.

Most libraries have a collection of basic bibliographic materials you can use to compile a list of books, pamphlets, and newspapers to be checked. Many of the materials so listed can then be obtained at the local library through inter-library loan services, or by visiting the institution where the materials are held. A good beginning reference to look for is the *Bibliography of Canadian Bibliographies* (2nd, rev. and enl. ed.) compiled by Douglas Lochhead. (Toronto: University of Toronto Press, 1972). This text contains a list of bibliographic materials related wholly or principally to Canada, arranged by subject. Bibliographies on Canadian railways, early newspaper directories, pottery and ceramics in Canada, interior decoration, provincial and federal government departmental

Plate 3.1. Exhibition certificate awarded to J. Ahrens, a Paris, Ontario, potter. Records of exhibitors to international, national, and provincial exhibitions are a source of information on industrial activity and the quality of Canadian products. Courtesy Brant County Museum, Brantford, Ontario

publications, and personal travel accounts and diaries are included.

Library research should give you a preliminary bibliography of resource material important to your research project, and a start on the study of material available locally. It will soon become evident that a great number of interesting documents have been lost, due either to the owners' indifference, or to destruction by fire or flooding. These three villains have been responsible for the loss of much of our primary historical resource material.

Besides the local library, other sources of local historical information are the proceedings of municipal and township councils, local church or synagogue records, tax assessment books, land-registry office books, fire insurance maps and plans, petitions to local government bodies, records of fraternal societies, local museums, cemetery boards, and the local or regional engineering road or planning board records. Many local historical records held by organizations or individuals are available to a researcher who takes the time and energy to find them.

In this brief introduction to the wealth of community resources available to the researcher, it is not possible to give complete details on all the types of information. The three basic sources of information in the local community, however, will be dealt with in some depth. These are the local and regional histories, church records, and newspapers and periodicals.

Local and Regional Histories

Read the available local history works for an over-view of the history of the area. Very few parts of Canada are without at least one such book or manuscript, describing the early settlers, churches, businesses and traditions. A word of caution, however. The quality and accuracy of these writings vary with the training and experience of the author: accept nothing in them verbatim. Information in local histories should be used only after having been independently assessed. (Unfortunately, many local histories do not indicate their sources.)

Local community libraries usually have copies of historical writings, whether printed or in manuscript form. There are bibliographies of local or regional history works to consult for materials that may be unavailable or unknown to the local library. A good bibliography for the Atlantic Provinces is William F. Morley, *The Atlantic Provinces: Newfoundland, Nova Scotia, New Brunswick, Prince Edward Island.* (Toronto: University of Toronto Press, 1967). This is the first volume of the series *Canadian Local Histories to 1950: A Bibliography.* The second volume, by André Beaulieu, is *La Province de Québec* (Toronto: University of Toronto Press, 1971), dealing with Quebec local history. The third volume of the series includes Ontario and the Canadian North and has not yet been published.

The publication *Canadiana*, begun in 1951 and published monthly, is Canada's official national bibliography and records all current items of Canadiana including books, pamphlets, microfilms, films and filmstrips, and federal government publications. *Canadiana* provides information on publications issued after other bibliographies. The *Bibliographie du Québec*, begun in 1969 by the National Library of Quebec, is a quarterly list of all books published in Quebec, all French language publications issued elsewhere in Canada, and all books of interest to Quebec that have been published outside Canada.

Local histories for the Province of Ontario are listed in Barbara Aitkin, *Local histories of Ontario municipalities, published in the years 1957-1972* (rev. and enl. ed. Kingston: Kingston Public Library Board, 1972), and the publication of the Ontario Department of Municipal Affairs titled *Local histories of municipalities.* For research concerning Western Ontario there is Olga Bishops' "Checklist of historical works on Western Ontario in the libraries of the University of Western Ontario" in *Western Ontario Historical Notes*, published in 1957 and 1958. A bibliography of books, periodical literature, and government reports related to Northern Ontario has been published as *Northern Ontario; a bibliography* (compiled by Loraine Spencer and Susan Holland. Toronto: University of Toronto Press, 1968.).

Reference guides for local histories of Western Canada are included in Bruce B. Peel, *A bibliography of the Prairie Provinces to 1953* (Toronto: University of Toronto Press, 1956), and its *Supplement*, published in 1963. For local history writing in British Columbia there is Barbara Lowther, *A bibliography of British Columbia; laying the foundations, 1848-1899* (Victoria, B.C.: University of Victoria, 1968), and *Navigations, traffiques & discoveries, 1774-1848; a guide to publications relating to the area now British Columbia* (compiled by Gloria M. Stathern, with the assistance of Margaret Edwards. Victoria, B.C.: Social Sciences Research Centre, 1970).

The *Canadian Periodical Index*, the *Canadian Historical Review* and *Ontario History* maintain up-to-date yearly indexes to articles on Canadian history, local history, and economic history. These are convenient sources for information on the most recent writings in each locality. For articles on French-American history, the researcher should consult the issues of *Revue d'histoire de l'amerique française*, published by the Institut d'histoire de l'Amerique française, Montreal.

Church Records

Important data for the study of early migrations to Canada can be found in church records. These records yield dates of church buildings, settlements or industries established by religious denominations; family relationships; and information on births, baptisms, marriages and burials. Records of ecclesiastical decisions affecting the life of the community may also be included, and some church records contain vivid

first-hand accounts of life in Canada as experienced by early missionaries.

Like many local government documents,
church records have been the victims of time.
Many early manuscripts are squirrelled away in
filing cabinets or desk drawers, difficult to locate
and to obtain access to. Some of the smaller con-
gregations may send their records to regional
conference, diocese, or convention headquarters,
or to national church archives. If you are studying the history of a particular person or family,
first find out the name and denomination of the
parish to which the family belonged. Then write
to the local clergyman. He will then be able to
make inquiries to locate books or records. Many
religious groups consider their records pri-
vileged information and restrict access to them.
In these cases you may have to request in writing the exact information required, indicating its
proposed use.

These are the national archives of some of the
larger religious denominations:

United Church of Canada Archives
Victoria University
Queen's Park
Toronto, Ontario

Mennonite Archives
Conrad Grebel College
University of Waterloo
Waterloo, Ontario

Anglican Church of Canada
General Synod Archives
Church House
600 Jarvis Street
Toronto, Ontario

Evangelical Lutheran Synod of Canada Archives
The Library
Wilfrid Laurier University
Waterloo, Ontario

Archives of the Religious Society of Friends
(Quakers)
The Library
University of Western Ontario
London, Ontario

Presbyterian Archives
Knox College
Caven Library
59 St. George St.
Toronto, Ontario

Canadian Baptist Archives
McMaster Divinity College
Hamilton, Ontario

In some cases parish churches may have retained extensive records, such as registers of
baptisms, marriages and deaths. A useful
bibliography of books, articles, congregation and
parish histories is Michael Sheehan, "A current
bibliography of Canadian church history", in
the 1964 issue of the *Report* of the Canadian
Catholic Historical Association.

In addition to the actual archives, there are
several bibliographies that may help to locate
material dealing with Jewish history. Among
them are *Canadian Jewish archives; list of documents and material* (Montreal: Canadian Jewish
Congress, 1939); Raymond A. Davies, *Printed
Jewish Canadiana, 1685-1900...*, (Montreal:
Davies, 1955), and David Rome, *...A selected
bibliography of Jewish Canadiana* (Montreal:
Canadian Jewish Congress and the Jewish
Public Library, 1959).

A useful bibliography on Doukhobors is
Maria Horvath, *A Doukhobor Bibliography...* (Vancouver: University of British Columbia, 1968). Information on the Hutterites
may be found in Ruth McIntyre, *The Hutterites in
North America; a bibliography of the resources
available in the Toronto Public Library and the Library of the University of Toronto,* (Unpublished
manuscript, U. of T. Library School 1966). A list
of the archives of the Religious Society of
Friends (Quakers) in Canada is available from
the Canadian Friends Historical Association,
Toronto.

The *Journal* of the Canadian Church Historical
Society contains useful notes and information
about local and national church history.

Newspapers and Periodicals

Most nineteenth-century towns of any size had
their own newspapers, some of which still appear. Old newspapers are gold mines of information about local events, industries, buildings
and people. A visit to a newspaper office may be
a help in your search for information, as many
papers maintain sets of back issues and possibly
clipping files. Most of the early newspapers were

only four or six pages long, and the print was small and crowded. Nor was the layout what we are used to now. You will need plenty of time and a careful eye to locate the small items that may be clues to the people or events you are trying to trace.

Many early newspaper publishers also did commercial printing. Copies of price lists, photographs, and other samples of material relating to early industry and events are occasionally found in old print shop records.

If you don't know whether a newspaper existed in a particular area, or the location of holdings of these early papers, consult *American Newspapers, 1821-1936; a union list of files available in the United States and Canada.* (New York: H.W. Wilson, 1937. Reprinted by Kraus Reprint Corp., N.Y., 1967). This comprehensive list of U.S. and Canadian newspapers is compiled geographically by place of publication, and lists the present location of back issues. Other aids for locating local newspapers are André Beaulieu, *Les journaux du Québec de 1764 à 1964* (Quebec: L'Institut d'histoire), and Edith G. Firth, *Early Toronto Newspapers 1793-1867. A catalogue of newspapers published in the Town of York and the City of Toronto from the beginning to Confederation* (Toronto: Baxter Publishing Co., 1961). There are also directories of early newspapers for the Provinces of New Brunswick, Nova Scotia, Manitoba and Saskatchewan. For New Brunswick papers, consult J. Russell Harper, *Historical directory of New Brunswick newspapers and periodicals.* (Fredericton: University of New Brunswick, *ca.* 1961). For Nova Scotia see Grace Tratt, *Check list of Canadian small presses, English language* (Halifax: Dalhousie University Libraries and Dalhousie University School of Library Science, 1974). Manitoba newspapers are listed in Maurice Pratt, *The story of Manitoba's weekly newspapers* (Winnipeg: Manitoba Newspaper Association, 1968). Saskatchewan newspapers are listed in Christine MacDonald, *Historical directory of Saskatchewan newspapers, 1878-1950* (Saskatoon: Office of the Saskatchewan Archives, University of Saskatchewan, 1951). For a convenient but dated survey of the newspaper files in Western Ontario see "A Checklist of early newspaper files located in local newspa-

per offices in Western Ontario" in *Western Ontario History Nuggets* No. 12, 1947.

The Microfilm Committee of the Canadian Library Association has been microfilming newspapers so that positive copies of the microfilms can be made available in local libraries. A list of Canadian newspapers microfilmed in this project is given in *Canadian newspapers on microfilm* (Ottawa: Canadian Library Assn., 1959 3v). Each newspaper microfilmed is listed by place of publication. A brief history of the newspaper, including publisher, editors, and editorial policies is included in the listing. The work also includes a list of microfilmed Canadian newspapers other than those filmed by the Canadian Library Association.

Early Canadian publishing houses also produced periodicals, on agriculture, sports, domestic and household science, retail trade, fraternal societies and literature. Some of these periodicals were of interest only to the local or regional population, while others served a national audience. One national publication with a great deal of information on cities such as Montreal, Toronto and Quebec is the *Canadian Illustrated News*, which was published from 1870 to 1884.

For sources of information on Canadian periodicals, consult McKim's *Directory of Canadian publications*, first issued in 1892, and N.W. Ayer and Son's *Directory of newspapers and periodicals*, first published in 1880. Both of these directories give authoritative information on magazines and trade publications published in Canada, arranged by place of publication with an alphabetical index of titles.

THE USE OF ARCHIVAL COLLECTIONS

After you have exhausted the resources of public libraries, private ownership, businesses, and government offices, start investigating archives. As many documents of interest to the historical archaeologist may have been transferred from small towns or townships to regional depositories, you may have to spend a great deal more time in municipal, provincial or the Federal

Plate 3.2. Fort York from an 1841 engraving which appeared in the Canadian Illustrated News *shows the guard house (left inside of gate) which was to become the object of an archaeological investigation.*

archives than in the local community. Archival collections are usually housed in well equipped buildings, prepared to welcome visitors and to answer inquiries from those interested in using the materials. Municipal and provincial government archives frequently keep civic records, manuscripts concerning local families, photographs, city maps, plans and other local and regional documents. Many of these historical records are available on microfilm or can be photocopied for a nominal fee. The Public Archives of Canada, Ottawa, has a comprehensive collection of original documents, drawings, watercolours, maps, photographs, and other Canadiana. The Public Archives produces a number of bibliographies of interest to the researcher, including the *Union List of Manuscripts in Canadian Repositories* (rev. and enl. ed., 1975), a comprehensive list of all significant manuscript groups in archival institutions in Canada, and a series of preliminary invento-

ries of manuscript groups relating to Canadian history. These preliminary inventories provide a general introduction and description of primary source materials, either in the Public Archives or in collections the Archives has photostated or microfilmed. The preliminary inventories include documents of importance to Canadian history in the Archives Nationales of Paris, the Colonial Office Papers in the Public Record Office, London, transcripts of papers in the British Museum, and many other documents on eighteenth and nineteenth-century Canada held in the Public Archives, Manuscript Division. In 1971 the Public Archives began a *General Inventory* of all documents in their manuscript division, which will update and complete the preliminary series. A supplementary series listing holdings of early official records of the Government of Canada was begun in 1953. The annual *Report* of the Archivist, begun in 1872, although primarily a report of the activities of the institution, occasionally contains lists of books, pamphlets, maps, charts and calendars of documents contained in the archives.

The Public Archives publishes a number of brochures giving concise information on the organization and services of the institution. These brochures are available without cost from Ottawa. One of these, *The Archivist*, published six times a year by the Public Archives, describes the activities of the institution and recent publications of interest to persons using archival collections.

Each province has its own archives, containing large collections of manuscripts and other records related to the province as a whole. Quite frequently town records no longer of use in the day-to-day working of local government are deposited in provincial archives. They may also be available on microfilm. The provincial archives are:

Provincial Museum and Archives of Alberta
12845 - 102 Avenue
Edmonton, Alberta

Provincial Archives of British Columbia
Parliament Buildings
Victoria, British Columbia

Provincial Archives of Manitoba
247 Legislative Building
Winnipeg, Manitoba

Department of Canadian History
Archives Division
New Brunswick Museum
St. John, New Brunswick

Provincial Archives of Newfoundland and Labrador
Colonial Building
Military Road
St. John's, Newfoundland

Public Archives of Nova Scotia
Dalhousie University
Studley Campus
Coburg Rd.
Halifax, Nova Scotia

Archives of Ontario
77 Grenville St.
Queen's Park
Toronto, Ontario

Public Archives of P.E.I.
Legislative Building
Charlottetown, Prince Edward Island

Archives Nationales du Québec
Parc des Champs de Bataille
Québec, Quebéc

Saskatchewan Archives Board
Legislative Library
Regina, Saskatchewan

The best way to determine the holdings of a provincial archive is to visit the institution yourself and consult the guides to the collections. If you can't make the trip, a written inquiry will usually bring a helpful answer. Published bibliographies of holdings of the provincial archives include:

British Columbia

Dictionary catalogue of the Library of the Provincial Archives of British Columbia. (Boston: G.K. Hall, 1971, 8 v.).

Manitoba

Public Archives of Manitoba. Preliminary inventory 1955. (Winnipeg: Legislative Library, 1955).

New Brunswick

Inventory of Manuscripts. (St. John: New Brunswick Museum, 1967).

Nova Scotia

A catalogue of maps, plans and charts in the public archives of Nova Scotia. Compiled by Marion Gilroy. (Halifax: Public Archives, 1938).
Phyllis Blakeley. "Archival Sources for Historical Research" in The *Occasional*, (Halifax, vol. 12, No. 2, 1974).

Ontario

Report of the archivist. Toronto, Ontario vol. 1- 1903.

Quebec

État général des archives publiques et privées. Quebec: Ministère des affaires culturelles, 1968.
Rapport des archives. tome 1- 1956.

Saskatchewan

Report of the Saskatchewan Archives. 1st- 1946.

City archives can give you civic records, manuscripts on local families and events, photographs, city maps, and plans. They will have many kinds of material on microfilm. Larger cities like Edmonton, Vancouver and Toronto have municipal archives with extensive holdings of records directly related to their own jurisdictions, as well as to many of the surrounding communities. The addresses of these archives are:

City of Edmonton Archives
10105 - 112 Avenue
Edmonton, Alberta

Vancouver City Archives
1150 Chestnut Street
Vancouver, B.C.

City of Toronto Archives
City Hall
Toronto, Ontario

There are archival collections in larger city libraries, private companies, and in university collections. The Toronto Public Library has a large collection of Canadiana, listed in a number of bibliographies including *Guide to the manuscript collection in the Toronto Public Libraries* (enl. ed. Prepared by Donalda Putnam and Edith Firth, 1954). St. Francis Xavier University, Sydney, N.S. has an extensive *Cape Bretoniana Archives*, consisting of historic records, maps, newspapers and oral history materials concerning Cape Breton, Nova Scotia.

Once you know the variety of historical documents available, your next task is to discover what records of interest to you have survived. The history of an area can be understood only within the framework of its geography, demography, economy and political organization. In building such a factual framework, you will find important information in land title records, tax assessment records, census reports, county atlases, and provincial, city and town directories. If adequate records are not available in archival collections, either they have been destroyed or they are still in the local community.

Land-title Records

Land-title records are found in the county registry office. Today, they are used most frequently by lawyers who wish to certify that the owner of a piece of land has a marketable title to it. For historians, these records help in tracing actual ownership. In studying the history of a site, especially a house or industry, it is essential to establish the record of ownership during the period being studied. The date on which a particular piece of land was purchased by a potter or a brewer, for instance, may not be the earliest date on which a pottery or brewery was operating there. So, trace the title as far back as possible in order to reconstruct the complete history of a site accurately.

Proper use of land-title books requires a basic understanding of how land was surveyed, settled, and recorded in government records. Using Upper Canada as a typical example, (although there was never complete uniformity of practice), this process will be briefly explained.

Laying out land through an established method of division into blocks and lots ensured a more orderly system of land transfer than squatting or settlement of unsurveyed parcels would have produced. After the land was "purchased" from the Indians, it was divided into townships, usually rectangular areas of land 9 miles wide by 12 miles deep, or 10 miles square. The earliest townships were laid out along river fronts and as a result did not have even boundaries. Inland, the township unit was divided into ranges or concessions, each concession being further divided into parcels of 100 or 200 acres. A road allowance was provided, at least in theory, in front of each concession or every second concession with a side road every half mile. Despite numerous changes in the regulations on surveying and obtaining land, and great variations in lot size, due to local conditions, a more or less regular system of surveyed townships, concessions and lots prevails over much of Canada and forms the framework on which an orderly system of land transfer has evolved.

Anyone planning to settle on land would petition the Governor-in-Council of the province for a grant. These petitions were often supported by documents from the petitioner's country of origin, testifying to his industriousness and integrity. Such documents gave details of the applicant's family and district of origin, and might also include testimonials of military or any other service to the Crown that might favourably influence the government. An Order-in-Council

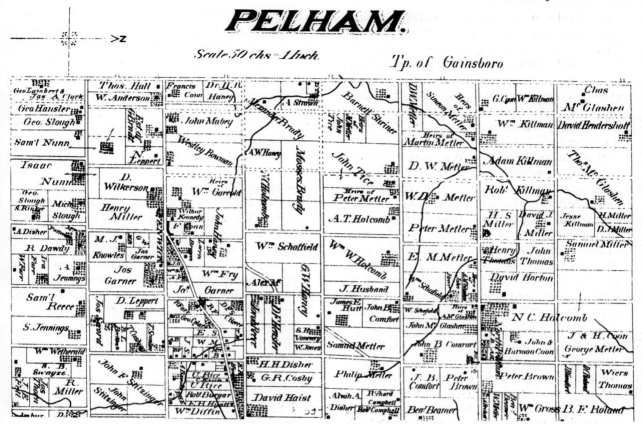

Plate 3.3. Historical atlases give information about land ownership, distribution and use at the time of the publication of the atlas.

approving a grant stated the quantity of land granted. When the land was paid for the settler was given a *warranty of survey* stating this amount. He would then take this document to the Surveyor-General's office and choose a vacant surveyed lot. His choice was entered in the plan of the township and in the government record book. The settler was given a *certificate of occupation,* later called a *location ticket.* He then had to find the lot and perform the *settlement duty* that entitled him to confirm his grant. This duty varied according to the legislation in force in the area of settlement. It usually involved building a house, occupying it with a family within a specified period of time, clearing and fencing a specified number of acres for agriculture, and clearing part of the road allowance in front of the holding. To obtain a deed to his land a settler had to prove that he had completed his settlement duty and that he

had taken an oath (or affirmation) of allegiance to the Crown before a magistrate. It was also important that he see that the land was properly described in the records at the Surveyor-General's office so that a deed could be prepared. (There were certain notable exceptions to this procedure, almost all of which involved the purchase of land from a land company, such as the Talbot Settlement or the Canada Company.) When all the land in a township was allocated, then the normal way of obtaining title to a parcel was to purchase it from the owner. Land close to Toronto and Montreal became settled at an early date and the only way to obtain crown land was to locate at greater distances from centres of growth.

Land allotment procedures varied greatly in the other provinces of Canada, due to the topography, the demand for land by settlers, and the influence of the railways on town sites. In

Newfoundland the settlers established themselves on land on a first-come basis, and only later did they call in a government surveyor. In Nova Scotia the land allotment procedures were complicated by the need to make sure that a grant was not part of the King's Woods, land set aside for naval purposes. A prospective settler petitioned the Governor for a grant. If the petition was initialed by the Governor, it was sent with a warrant or order to the Surveyor-General who was then to survey a tract of land of the designated size. When the parcel was surveyed, a description of the land was sent to the Governor, with a copy of the surveyor's report to the Surveyor-General of the King's Woods. A certificate of the Surveyor-General of the King's Woods was then sent with the warrant to survey and the surveyor's report to the Provincial Secretary's office, where the grant was made, and signed by the Governor.

In New Brunswick the regulations of 1785 stipulated that after a number of farms had been surveyed, settlers who wanted a parcel of land were to draw lots, under the supervision of the Deputy Surveyor. Successful settlers were then issued a certificate of possession. The Deputy Surveyor was then responsible for showing the prospective settler his lot, and reporting back to the Provincial Secretary.

More or less regular patterns of land settlement prevailed in the west, although the lot size could vary considerably. Another influence in the settlement of the west was the Canadian Pacific Railway, which set out town sites and sold lots from the land originally granted to it by Parliament. Early settlement maps, to be discussed later in this chapter, may help to locate a specific grant.

Petitions for crown grants in Lower and Upper Canada before Confederation are in the custody of the Public Archives of Canada. At Confederation crown lands became a provincial responsibility and these records are now in the custody of the provincial governments. The Upper Canada land petitions are available on microfilm at the Ontario Archives. For Quebec land petitions, the National Archives of Quebec has large holdings of petitions and assignments of lots for the period 1788-1900 and petitions for land by militiamen for military service

(1812-1851). The Public Archives of Nova Scotia has the records of all petitions for land in that Province prior to Confederation. In Saskatchewan the records of applications for patent are filed at the Saskatchewan Archives Board, Saskatoon Office. Records of grants or *patents* of land are also available in provincial government offices, or in archival collections, where they are usually filed according to township. A brief list of the provincial authorities concerned with land grants is found in the pamphlet, *Tracing Your Ancestors in Canada* (Ottawa: Public Archives of Canada, 1972). Archival institutions such as the Public Archives of Nova Scotia and the Saskatchewan Archives Board have card indexes to the names and locations of all settlers in their provinces. Keep in mind, however, that a settler might obtain a certificate of occupation and actually live and farm on a piece of land before filing for a deed. Settlers often obtained legal title to their grants only when sale or subdivision of the land seemed likely.

In most provinces the provincial government was responsible only for the initial recording of land grants; records of all subsequent subdivisions and sale of property were entered in the copy book of deeds in the county in which the property was located. The early registers of deeds and land transactions (called abstract books) for Ontario are on microfilm at the Provincial Archives. For other provinces, go to the county or area registry office. Land title registrars, or deed registrars, are listed by province in the annual issues of the *Canadian Almanac and Directory* (Toronto: Copp Clark Publishing Company).

The abstract book lists the dates of sale of the property, the names of people involved, amount of any mortgage, the sale price, and any liens on the property. Documents for each of these transactions, called *instruments*, are registered and numbered. There is a great deal to be learned from examining these instruments. Since they give exact boundaries and precise details of the property, they are important in defining the limits of a site. They may also include information on the name, occupation, literacy and offspring of the purchaser. All these details are helpful in reconstructing the lives of the site's inhabitants.

In Quebec the search for property records becomes more complicated. All property transactions, wills, and inventories were recorded by a notary and the records in the registry offices are kept under the notary's name. The inventories of notarial records are simply chronological abstracts, naming the type of transaction, the date and the names of the people involved. They do not give the location of the land affected, and this must be found by consulting the relevant document. If several notaries worked in one district, the inventories of all notary records for the period have to be checked. Any enquiry may be further complicated by the possibility that the transaction may not have been registered in the district but in Montreal or Quebec, on a trip to town. Published inventories of notary records have been issued for the city of Quebec and for some of the Montreal notaries.

In other provinces, the same type of record exists as in Ontario, although the abstract books may not deal with specific counties.

Tax Assessment Records

All properties within a particular municipality were assessed yearly for tax purposes. The information recorded varies from one province to another. It may include the name of the owner or the head of the household occupying the property, his age, religion, occupation, and the number of people resident. Such data helps to complete the picture of household units, trace property values, and define the social and family situation of individuals who lived on the site. The assessment records are located in the office of the municipal or town clerk. Some of the earlier records have been microfilmed and may be available in archival collections.

Nominal Census

The nominal census, a list of individuals and households, is one of the most valuable sources of information about people and occupations in the nineteenth century. The census for 1851 and onwards lists individuals by name, age, sex, birthplace, religion, racial origin, occupation, marital status, education, and birth or death in the year. The description of households states the kind of house occupied, distinguishes relatives from non-relatives, and gives a general indication of the relationship of members in each household. In instances where the head of the household was engaged in business the census gives the store or shop owner, number of people employed, and other details.

The earliest known nominal census was taken in New France in 1666. There were many others in the succeeding centuries; three have been preserved from the seventeenth. These early censuses give the names of husband and wife, their age, the names of each of their children, and their property. In 1842 the united province of Upper and Lower Canada passed the first census act, and from 1851 onward a ten-year census interval became an established practice. In the west, however, a census was taken in Manitoba in 1886 and both Alberta and Saskatchewan conducted one in 1905, thereby establishing a practice of a five-year census midway between the ten-year census.

The censuses for 1851 through 1871 are available on microfilm from the Public Archives of Canada, or in provincial archives for the microfilms pertaining to each province. The federal government has not released nominal census records after 1871.

County Atlases

The first Canadian county atlas was produced in 1874, and for the next decade a series of these historical atlases was produced for sale in rural Canada. Twelve "Dominion of Canada" atlases with individual county supplements were also produced during this period.

A county atlas was financed by subscription. Salesmen would go from town to town selling the atlas by contract, usually charging the customer anywhere from six to ten dollars a copy. Prominent people could have their biography included for another ten dollars; a sketch of a property would cost about fifty dollars. Because of the need to sell subscriptions, atlases were produced only for counties where the population was large enough to make the venture profitable for the publisher. Accordingly, the county atlases cover mainly southern Ontario and the Maritimes. By 1910 the interest in atlas publishing had declined and areas of Canada settled later were never included in any historical atlas.

Atlas publishers did not always do local field research and therefore are not necessarily an independent source of information. In some instances the publishers appear to have used information from Crown land and county assessment offices. A recent study of the historical atlas of Pictou County, Nova Scotia has shown that the atlas is an accurate historical document of most land-holdings at the time it was produced, in 1879. In general, however, atlases do not show all the small-sized farms and businesses, or if these do appear, the owner's name does not. County atlases are especially useful as corroboration of information from land registry offices, tax assessment records and the census, in drawing a profile of the people and industries of a particular area.

The *Illustrated Historical Atlas of the County of Brant, Ontario*, published in 1875, is a typical county atlas of the day. It includes an historical sketch of the county, a business directory, and a series of maps. The first set of maps is of the Maritimes, eastern Quebec, western Quebec and Ontario. These are followed by township maps and eighteen maps of municipalities, indicating land-holdings at the time the atlas was compiled. Illustrations include lithographs of the public buildings, churches, the YMCA, the Court House, the Registry Office, and the Council House of the Six Nations Indians. Other lithographs show prominent businesses of the county, views of houses, and the countryside. Finally there are six pages of business cards and

Plate 3.4a. Advertising for the W.E. Welding Stoneware factory from an 1875 historical atlas of Brant County, Ontario.

advertising. One lithograph is of the W.E. Welding stoneware factory. For a time, this was the only known view of the second building of the firm, built in 1873, and was of great assistance in determining areas to dig during rescue excavations in the winter of 1966. The atlas view of the factory was included in the published report of the excavations.

A descriptive catalogue of the county atlases has been prepared by Miss Betty May and was

Plate 3.4b. Bird's-eye view map of the Brantford Stoneware factory, Brantford, Ontario. The maps are drawn from above at an oblique angle, and show individual buildings, streets and landscape features in perspective.

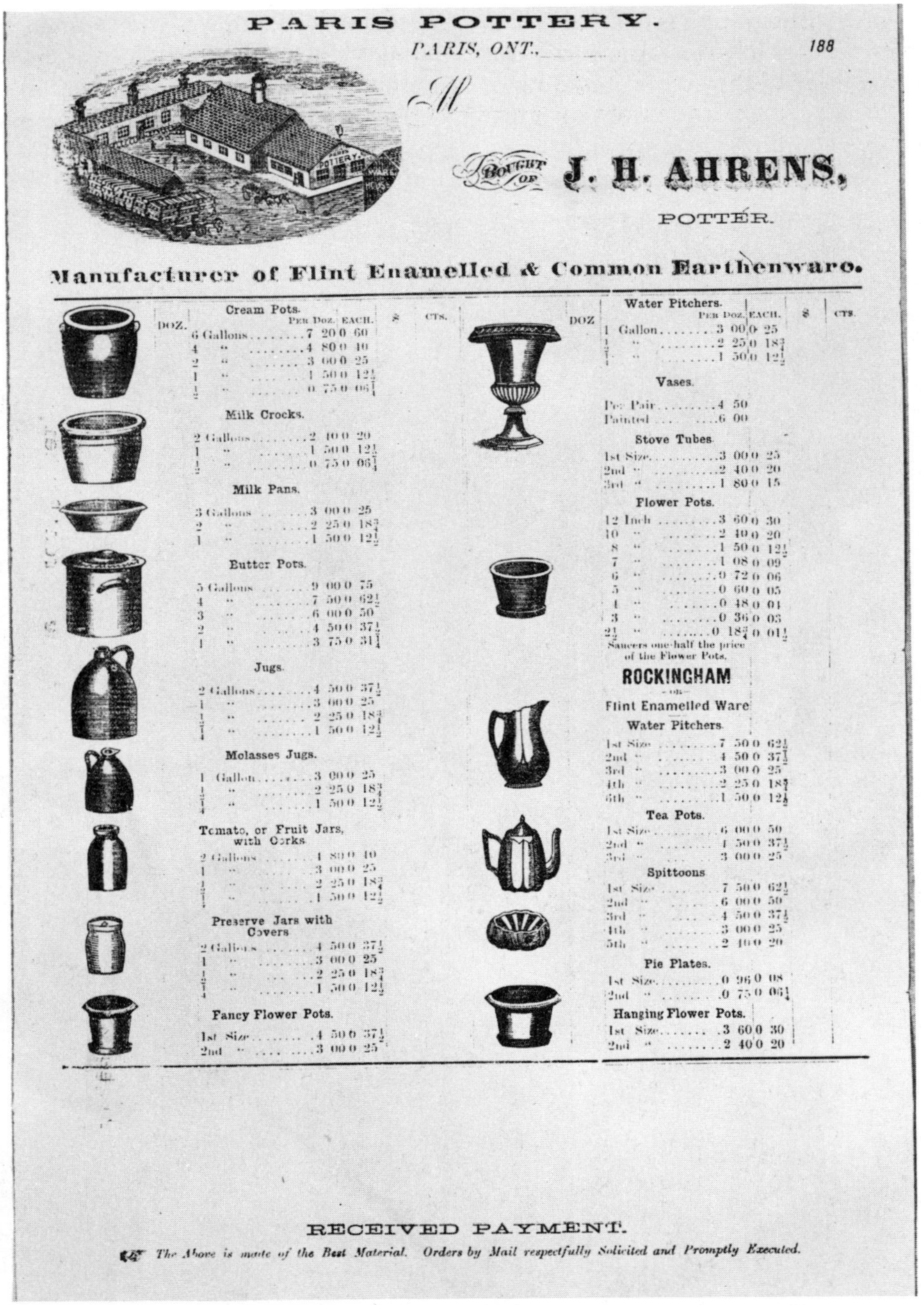

PARIS POTTERY.

PARIS, ONT., ________ 188

M

Bought of J. H. AHRENS, POTTER.

Manufacturer of Flint Enamelled & Common Earthenware.

DOZ.		Per Doz.	Each.	$	Cts.
	Cream Pots.				
	6 Gallons	7 20	0 60		
	4 "	4 80	0 40		
	2 "	3 00	0 25		
	1 "	1 50	0 12½		
	½ "	0 75	0 06¼		
	Milk Crocks.				
	2 Gallons	2 40	0 20		
	1 "	1 50	0 12½		
	½ "	0 75	0 06¼		
	Milk Pans.				
	3 Gallons	3 00	0 25		
	2 "	2 25	0 18¾		
	1 "	1 50	0 12½		
	Butter Pots.				
	5 Gallons	9 00	0 75		
	4 "	7 50	0 62½		
	3 "	6 00	0 50		
	2 "	4 50	0 37½		
	1 "	3 75	0 31¼		
	Jugs.				
	2 Gallons	4 50	0 37½		
	1 "	3 00	0 25		
	½ "	2 25	0 18¾		
	¼ "	1 50	0 12½		
	Molasses Jugs.				
	1 Gallon	3 00	0 25		
	½ "	2 25	0 18¾		
	¼ "	1 50	0 12½		
	Tomato, or Fruit Jars, with Corks				
	2 Gallons	4 80	0 40		
	1 "	3 00	0 25		
	½ "	2 25	0 18¾		
	¼ "	1 50	0 12½		
	Preserve Jars with Covers				
	2 Gallons	4 50	0 37½		
	1 "	3 00	0 25		
	½ "	2 25	0 18¾		
	¼ "	1 50	0 12½		
	Fancy Flower Pots.				
	1st Size	4 50	0 37½		
	2nd "	3 00	0 25		

DOZ		Per Doz.	Each.	$	Cts.
	Water Pitchers.				
	1 Gallon	3 00	0 25		
	½ "	2 25	0 18¾		
	¼ "	1 50	0 12½		
	Vases.				
	Per Pair	4 50			
	Painted	6 00			
	Stove Tubes.				
	1st Size	3 00	0 25		
	2nd "	2 40	0 20		
	3rd "	1 80	0 15		
	Flower Pots.				
	12 Inch	3 60	0 30		
	10 "	2 40	0 20		
	8 "	1 50	0 12½		
	7 "	1 08	0 09		
	6 "	0 72	0 06		
	5 "	0 60	0 05		
	4 "	0 48	0 04		
	3 "	0 36	0 03		
	2½ "	0 18¾	0 01½		
	Saucers one-half the price of the Flower Pots.				
	ROCKINGHAM — OR — Flint Enamelled Ware				
	Water Pitchers.				
	1st Size	7 50	0 62½		
	2nd "	4 50	0 37½		
	3rd "	3 00	0 25		
	4th "	2 25	0 18¾		
	6th "	1 50	0 12½		
	Tea Pots.				
	1st Size	6 00	0 50		
	2nd "	4 50	0 37½		
	3rd "	3 00	0 25		
	Spittoons				
	1st Size	7 50	0 62½		
	2nd "	6 00	0 50		
	3rd "	4 50	0 37½		
	4th "	3 00	0 25		
	5th "	2 40	0 20		
	Pie Plates.				
	1st Size	0 96	0 08		
	2nd "	0 75	0 06¼		
	Hanging Flower Pots.				
	1st Size	3 60	0 30		
	2nd "	2 40	0 20		

RECEIVED PAYMENT.

The Above is made of the Best Material. Orders by Mail respectfully Solicited and Promptly Executed.

Plate 3.5. A price list of products available at the J. H. Ahrens Pottery, Paris, Ontario. Business records of potteries give not only the price but also tell the researcher something of the pottery shapes, sizes and functions. Courtesy Brant County Museum, Brantford, Ontario

published in 1970 under the title *County Atlases of Canada.* The publication is available from the National Map Collection of the Public Archives of Canada, Ottawa. Reports of current research on historical atlases and maps appear in the *Newsletter* and the *Proceedings* of the Association of Canadian Map Libraries. The publications of the Association first appeared in 1967 and information on back issues and subscriptions can be obtained from the Association, c/o National Map Collection of the Public Archives of Canada.

Directories

Like county atlases, directories provide information on businesses and prominent individuals of different municipalities. The early directories contained an alphabetical list of the names of the residents of the city, town or township, and listed by street the individuals engaged in each of the local trades. Some contained a classified business directory, and occasionally a list of government departments, post offices, churches, doctors, schools, hotels, banks and popular societies of the day. In the late nineteenth century some directories included illustrations of buildings, a short history and description of businesses, and other useful commercial information. Canadian directories were published from 1851 onward, including Manitoba and Newfoundland by the 1880s.

Ontario had county, city and sometimes town directories. Over thirty were produced for York and Toronto during the nineteenth century. The earliest is the *York commercial directory, street guide and register*, published in 1833, which contains an alphabetical list of names and a directory of streets. An annotated list of York and Toronto directories is found in Jean McFall's "Early Directories of Toronto and York," published in the *York Pioneer* for 1955. Two useful bibliographies of directories are P.L. Fleming, "A bibliography of Ontario directories in 1867," *Ontario Library Review,* June 1975 and R.B. Land, "City directories; bibliography," in *Canadian Business,* April 1958. Check federal and provincial archives for directories in their collections.

There are a great number of other sources of information valuable to you as an archaeologist. For example:

Early Maps

Early maps preserve information on the landscape, including the use of land and its ownership. There are settlement maps, showing the areas laid out for farming and townsites and parcels taken up and reserved, early general maps of provinces and territories indicating the location of towns, roads and post offices, maps prepared by French and English military forces for campaign purposes, and street maps of cities and towns, with street patterns and major landscape features. These are but a few of the large variety of maps and plans available in collections.

Settlement maps were produced at the time a purchase was laid out and made available for settlement. The field books, journals and other notes of the land surveyor were submitted to the provincial Surveyor-General's office as soon as possible after the completion of a survey. From these records a manuscript describing the land and a map showing townships, concessions and lots would be produced. As lots were taken up the settlers' names were added to the map. These early Surveyor-General's maps also showed districts, counties, townships, main villages, towns and Indian settlements.

One example of a settlement map is Samuel Holland's *Province of Lower Canada*, a map showing seigneuries, townships and land grants according to the plans of the patent office in Quebec. In Upper Canada (Ontario) the early Surveyors-General D.W. Smyth, W. Chewett, and T. Rideout all produced settlement maps. Other, large-scale maps, were produced in the 1860s by the map-making firms of Tackabury and Tremaine. These were drawn at 5 or 6 miles to the inch, and show churches, schools and post offices.

An 1873 land office map for the Province of Manitoba shows lands laid out for settlement and those taken up and reserved. The area is shown as described in the first survey of the Selkirk colony, which was laid out along the Red River in 1813. (Subsequent surveys used different systems, such as the rectangular township.)

Admiralty maps and charts are other sources of settlement information. Although prepared primarily to show the sea bottom near the coast, they also include the location of coastal settlements and often the main structures in these settlements.

Useful for urban areas, and therefore of primary interest to the archaeologist studying industrial sites, are panoramic or bird's eye view maps. These present a view of the city from above at an oblique angle. They reproduce the street patterns, individual lots and buildings, and major landscape features. This mapping technique flourished from 1870 to 1910 and most larger cities had several editions during this period. In the National Map Collection of the Public Archives of Canada there are maps for cities such as Montreal, Ottawa, and Toronto.

There are many collections of maps, public, on the federal, provincial and municipal levels, and private. The Map Division, Public Archives of Canada, collects all original maps of Canada and now has more than three hundred thousand. Several catalogues of the collection have been published, including T.E. Layng, *Sixteenth-century maps relating to Canada* (Ottawa: Public Archives, 1956); P.E. Dumas, *Catalogue of seventeenth and eighteenth century maps relating to Canada.*

The Glenbow Foundation of Calgary maintains a collection of early maps of Alberta. The Provincial Museum and Archives, Edmonton, also acquires published and unpublished maps of Alberta prior to 1914.

The Map Division of the Provincial Archives of British Columbia, Victoria, and the Special Collections Division, The Library, University of British Columbia, Vancouver have large collections of early maps of British Columbia, Alaska, and the Yukon.

In Manitoba the Provincial Library and Archives has a collection of early maps of Manitoba and the Northwest Territories for the year 1800 onward. The maps issued after 1870 deal primarily with the surveying system and the growth of transport and communications.

The New Brunswick Museum holds a number of early maps of the province. The Archives Department, Bibliothèque Champlain, Université de Moncton, Moncton, has early maps of the Atlantic region and Canada, and specializes in maps and history of the Acadian region.

The Library of Memorial University, St. John's, has a small collection of early maps of Newfoundland and Labrador. These can be supplemented by the maps available at the Provincial Archives in St. John's.

The Public Archives of Nova Scotia holds early maps of that province. The collection is described in *Catalogue of maps, plans, and charts in the Public Archives of Nova Scotia*, published in 1938.

The Ontario Archives has township, urban, topographic, and railway maps, dating from 1760 to 1900. Special maps include those made for Thomas Talbot, the Canada Company, Simcoe maps and the Bayfield marine charts. The Surveys Section, Department of Lands and Forests, Province of Ontario has all survey records and field notes of Crown lands of Ontario, and surveys of improved roads, railways, townsites, mining locations, lake and river traverses, and all original township surveys of Ontario.

The City of Toronto Surveyor's Department has maps relating to Toronto from 1793 onward. The Baldwin Room of the Toronto Public Library also has an extensive collection of early maps of Toronto and district. The published catalogue of the library's collection is *Map collection of the Public Reference Library of the City of Toronto* (Toronto: Public Library, 1923).

The private collection of early maps of Canada owned by the MacDonald Ophthalmic Foundation of Toronto has been described in a series of catalogues published by the Royal Ontario Museum. These catalogues include *Discovery and mapping of Upper Canada*, published in 1967; *"Over the Rockies" the discovery of mapping of the Canadian west, 1700-1886*, published in 1956; *Canada on maps 1564-1616*, published in 1966; *Canontariana*, published in 1975.

For the Province of Quebec, maps can be found at the Départment des documents spéciaux, Bibliothèque nationale du Québec, Montreal, and at the Collection de Cartes, Archives du Québec, Ministère des Affaires Culturelles, Quebec. Both of these sources have collections of seventeenth and eighteenth century maps of all parts of Quebec. Other sources include Collection Gagnon, Bibliothèque municipale de Montréal and La Cartothèque, Bibliothèque générale, Université Laval, Québec. A guide to the collection at Université Laval has been issued and is revised annually.

The Saskatchewan Archives Board has a collection of early maps of Saskatchewan and the Northwest Territories to 1905. Cartographers represented in the collection include David Thompson, Alexander Henry, Arrowsmith, Hector and Blakiston.

Business Records

Larger businesses may have their own research library where historical information is on file. These company libraries are part of what are known as a community's special libraries. In Toronto, the local chapter of the Special Libraries Association has compiled a *Directory of special libraries in the Toronto area* that lists over two hundred and forty libraries, many of them company libraries. The directory gives their location, subjects of interest, special facilities and services provided for visitors. Anyone studying industrial history should also consult Moira Cartwright, *Special libraries in Canada, 1954-1966: an annotated bibliography* (Unpublished manuscript, University of Toronto Library School, 1967).

Inquiry at a business headquarters may produce information about extant early records, and their location if they are no longer in the company's possession. Most businesses will give you access to old records once you explain your purposes in examining them. The Public Archives of Canada has a business archives pro-

gramme, whose objectives are to organize and preserve the records of firms and individuals of inter-provincial, national or multi-national importance. There is no such programme for small businesses. Their records may be deposited in local libraries and municipal or provincial archives. A guide to the company records in the Toronto Public Library is *Early Canadian companies; a guide to sources of information in the Toronto Public Libraries on selected Canadian companies over 100 years old* (compiled by Barbara Byers and others, 1967).

There are a number of bibliographies devoted to industries of national importance. Railways were intimately involved in urban growth during the nineteenth century, and their records are a source of information on many smaller towns. Three bibliographies of materials dealing with railways are the *Bibliographical list of references to Canadian railways 1829-1939* (Compiled under the auspices of the Library of the Bureau of Statistics, Ottawa, 1938); *The Canadian National Railway, A selected bibliography on Canadian railways* (Montreal, 1965) and Mary McCormick, *Books and pamphlets relating to the Canadian Pacific*

Plate 3.6. Early government publications may contain pictures such as this one of the Huron Pottery, Egmondville, Ontario. Courtesy Ontario Ministry of Natural Resources

Railway in the Library of the Department of Transport, Ottawa (Unpublished manuscript, University of Ottawa Library School, 1960). For the iron and steel industry there is a dated but still useful book, William Donald, *The Canadian Iron and Steel Industry; a study in the economic history of a protected industry* (Boston: Houghton Mifflin Co., 1915).

FIRE INSURANCE MAPS AND PLANS

Between 1870 and 1930 a number of companies were actively producing maps and plans for insurance companies. These were used to determine insurance premiums on structures, and to show the location of water mains and fire-protection equipment. Most of these map-making companies were short-lived, with the exception of the Charles E. Goad firm, which produced maps for Canadian cities and smaller urban

centres from 1875 to 1910. The Goad maps were usually drawn on a scale of 50 feet to the inch, and used symbols and colours to show types of construction material, height, type of roof, and other architectural details of all buildings.

In 1973 the Map Division of the Public Archives of Canada obtained from the London, England office of the Goad company a collection of over one thousand plates and sheets covering cities such as Vancouver, Toronto, and Montreal, and over ninety smaller centres. The plans show individual enterprises such as warehouses, glass works, soap factories, and breweries. A guide to these insurance maps and plans is being prepared by the Public Archives.

The Insurers Advisory Organization, formerly the Canadian Underwriters' Association, which bought out the Goad company, has in its Toronto head office a complete file of all current fire insurance maps for some eleven hundred mu-

Plate 3.1. Painting of the nineteenth century pottery workshop of Jacob H. Ahrens, a contemporary record of the interior of an operating pottery giving much detail on building construction, pottery-making techniques, and shapes and uses of vessels. Courtesy Paris (Ontario) Public Library

nicipalities throughout Canada. The current map for some towns may be dated as far back as the 1890s, so it may be worthwhile to consult these files. Arrangements can be made to do so in the organization's office at 180 Dundas St. West, Toronto.

Early insurance maps and plans may also be found in municipal, provincial and special archives, engineering or fire departments, and city libraries. In the study of urban archaeology a fire insurance map or plan may provide information unavailable from any other source.

Federal, Provincial and Municipal Government Records

There are a large number of government publications dealing with all aspects of social, political and economic history. Because they present the work of a wide range of government departments, these publications can be extremely valuable. For example, the picture of the Huron Pottery, (plate 3.8) was found in an Ontario government publication on the clay industry, dated 1906. The same report gives a survey of the major brick yards, by county, a brief description of the porcelain, terra cotta and earthenware industry. Sources of clay, equipment used by the companies, and the quantity of bricks and tiles produced by each business are all detailed. Federal reports of the same period give additional information on the industry. In many instances there are later reports up-dating the earlier material. The 1906 report mentioned above was followed by reports in 1930 and 1967, providing valuable data on the brick and clay products industry. The reports are also useful for locating abandoned brickyards and for field surveys of kiln sites in the province.

Government publications deal with land settlement, early industry, postal services, mining and other industrial activity, health, and building construction, to name but a few. For the historical archaeologist the earlier reports are more descriptive and generally more useful. Useful guides to Federal government publications are Olga Bishop, *Publications of the government of the Province of Canada, 1841-1867* (Ottawa: Queen's Printer, 1963); *Publications of the Geological Surveys and National Museum 1909-1947* (Ottawa: Queen's Printer, 1948). For

provincial government publications refer to Mohan Bhatia, *Canadian provincial government publications; bibliography of bibliographies* (Rev. and enl. ed. Saskatoon: University of Saskatchewan Library, 1971). Important bibliographies for Ontario and Quebec are Hazel MacTaggart, *Publications of the government of Ontario 1901-1955. A checklist compiled for the Ontario Library Association.* (Toronto: University of Toronto Press for the Queen's Printer, 1964), and *Annotated list of publications of the Department of Mines of the province of Quebec 1883-1944* (Quebec: Paradis, Printer to the King, 1944).

Mercantile Reference Books

With the increase in business activity in the nineteenth century came a need for information about firms and individuals wishing to buy on credit. In 1841 the Mercantile Agency was founded by Lewis Tappen in New York, to provide detailed credit information for clients in the United States and Canada. The early reports, gathered by the company's agents, often commented on the marital status, family and ethnic background, age, former residence and business experience of all those requesting credit. The original Mercantile Agency expanded its activities during the nineteenth century and by 1859 was known as R.G. Dun & Company. Its only serious rival was the Bradstreet Agency, founded in 1849. In 1857 the first Bradstreet Agency reference or rating book was produced, followed two years later by the Mercantile Agency's first volume. The books contained the names of businesses, organized by city, an indentification of the type of business, and a numerical letter or code estimating the worth or credit standing of each entry. More detailed information on individuals and firms was retained by the company in its ledgers and was available to subscribers of the agency's services. Out-of-date books were returned to the company and destroyed. The two rival credit information agencies eventually merged to form Dun & Bradstreet. Over twenty-five hundred original ledgers of the Mercantile Agency and a large collection of papers relating to credit ratings are deposited in the Dun & Bradstreet Collection, Baker Library, Graduate School of Business Administration, Harvard University, U.S.A. In

Plate 3.8a. An old school photograph from Napanee, Ontario proved a valuable source of information on the nearby Napanee Glass Works. Courtesy Lennox & Addington Historical Society

Plate 3.8b. An enlargement of the right half of plate 3-8a shows the glass works in greater detail. This information proved to be valuable to the archaeologists digging at the glass site. Courtesy Lennox & Addington Historical Society

the study of early Canadian enterprise these records are a useful source of information on the growth of a particular firm or industry.

Personal Diaries and Travel Accounts

The first-hand impressions of travellers in Canada give vivid, if not always objective, views of living conditions in the past. References to transportation, social customs, individuals and local enterprise add the human dimension to what otherwise might be a catalogue of historical details and facts. A bibliography of both published and unpublished personal records is William Matthews (ed.), *Canadian diaries and autobiographies* (Berkeley, Calif.: University of California Press, 1950). For personal accounts of Upper Canada (Ontario) consult Ruth Tolmie, *Bibliography of personal accounts of travel in Upper Canada from the earliest years to 1833* (Unpublished manuscript, University of Toronto Library School, 1967), and Margaret S. Whiteside, *Upper Canada from the woman's view, a bibliography of journals, letters and books written by women travellers and settlers in Upper Canada 1767-1900* (Unpublished manuscript, University of Toronto Library School, 1966).

Miscellaneous Documentary Sources

Many other types of information can help in the study of an historical site—early paintings, for example, and illustrations or photographs depicting a subject at a known period. It may be worthwhile to investigate reports of provincial and local departments of health, the post and patent offices, annual reports of street railway companies, records of probated wills, and the reports of provincial, federal, and international exhibitions. Include military records, immigration records (especially from 1865 onward), and records of naturalization and citizenship. To those who become immersed in historical research, sources of information seem limited only by the time available and one's own re-

sourcefulness. Patience and initiative will reap rewards for the historical archaeologist who digs into the written sources as thoroughly as he does those below the ground.

Oral History Field Work

A researcher should interview anyone who might have personal information about a site. Oral history work can help in locating special features associated with a particular site, can provide human interest information about individuals or enterprises, and may give you further information on old papers, photographs or artifacts not in local or regional libraries or archival collections.

Two aspects of oral history work should be emphasized. First, it requires trained interviewers, able to gain the respect and confidence of the people to be interviewed. Older people do like to re-tell their experiences and enjoy an opportunity to share their past. The interviewer must be able to match their enthusiasm with patience, warmth, and a willingness to listen rather than do all the talking. There are any number of stories about untrained students descending on old peoples' homes and frightening the guests, or interrupting the narrative precisely when important information is being recounted. There are also accounts of senior citizens' groups themselves interviewing other senior citizens, and doing an excellent job. You might consider finding a versatile older person to do the interviewing involved in your project.

Your general area of interest and specific topics on which you want information could be supplied to him (or her). After evaluating the results of the first interview (which should be done with a portable cassette tape recorder) you can ask the interviewer to make a second visit to clarify or discuss material on the tapes. Oral history work should never be done in a hurry; don't rush or upset your informant.

A second point to remember about oral history work is that details and facts should always be confirmed through other known sources. Time and intervening events and experiences fade the memories of all but a few, and excessive reliance on interviews may lead to serious errors in historical judgement.

Chapter 4

THE FIELD SURVEY

The purpose of the field survey is to determine the exact location and condition of features of archaeological significance. Typical features are foundations of buildings, abandoned wells, remains of industrial structures, post holes, pits, fence lines, or areas of discoloured soil, brick, debris, or concentrations of artifacts. Any details confirming, completing or correcting the historical documentation of a site will contribute to the knowledge of what remains at the site and will help determine whether further archaeological investigation is merited.

The field survey may actually show that documentary evidence is incomplete or incorrect. For example, Canadian military forts were often constructed in haste, to meet a sudden threat to the country. Plans of forts may include not only buildings that actually existed at the time the plans were drawn, but also buildings which should have been built, or were incomplete. In some cases the buildings shown were never completed. Where questions arise about the existence of a particular building, a field survey may help to provide answers.

When a site is located it is necessary to take photographic records, in black and white and in colour, and to prepare sketches of the land and scaled plans of all above-ground structures. The field survey may also produce surface artifacts that hint at the range of materials to be found at the site, although don't assume that surface collections necessarily indicate what is below the ground. Frequently, surface artifacts are found

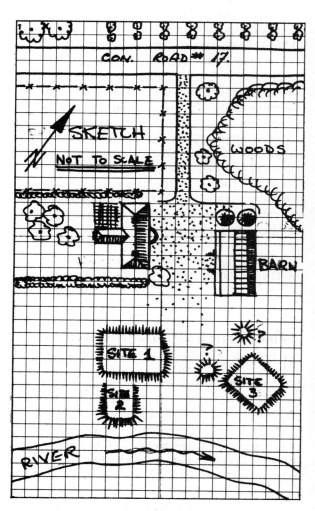

Figure 4.1. A simple sketch plan of a site.

to be stray discards by later visitors to the site, and do not indicate its use at an earlier date.

You may find that a detailed survey is all that is needed for your research plans. An accurate and complete survey can be a permanent contribution to our knowledge of historical sites and should be filed, or if possible published in an appropriate journal, so that the information will be readily available to future researchers. To help establish complete yet concise records, many individuals and organizations have developed their own field survey forms. This provides a standard format for survey information and, if properly organized may provide data that can be handled by electronic information retrieval systems.

If you are interested in the long-range archaeological potential of a site, a survey can provide an opportunity to learn the owner's short- and long-range land use plans. Any possibility that a site may be sold for development or that land-use patterns may change should be noted, as these alterations may result in the destruction of any remains of archaeological significance. On important sites the archaeological excavations should be timed to precede any major change in land-use.

It is important to remember that a field survey can only be completed by actually walking over a site, several times and from different directions, looking down and paying attention to what is under foot. You cannot do a survey from a slow-moving or parked automobile, or by aircraft; the detailed visual observations and surface collections can only be made on foot.

It is an essential prerequisite of all field survey work that the landowner or tenant give permission to walk over the site. This rule is not just a formality or a social nicety; it has legal and economic consequences. A landowner or tenant with a field under cultivation may ask that you examine it after the crop is harvested. Such a request may be to your advantage, as the surface of the ground will be more visible then. If a thoughtless field worker trespasses and damages crops or other objects, or injures livestock, or himself, he is likely to be involved in legal action. Field workers must keep in mind the need to solicit the cooperation of the public at all stages of investigation, not only for the success

of their own studies, but for the benefit of those workers who may follow them.

Provinces with legislation requiring a license for field survey work (see appendix) may require the written consent of the landowner as part of an application for a license. In these cases it will be necessary to communicate with landowners well in advance of the scheduled commencement of any full-scale field survey work. If your survey program is planned for the summer, get letters of permission from landowners in early spring of that year.

At your first meeting with the landowner or tenant you can explain the purpose of the survey and the site's historical and archaeological importance. This should dispel any fears that the owner may have concerning the nature of the investigation, and whether any damage will occur. Upon learning of your interest, the landowner may be able to point out significant features on the site or provide you with other information. He may also introduce you to people in the community who know more about the site. These first discussions with the landowner should determine the ownership of any surface artifacts that may be found. As a general rule the artifacts are the property of the landowner, but a sympathetic person will usually permit you to retain any artifacts found during the survey.

If the landowner will not relinquish rights to the artifacts, ask for permission to photograph and describe the surface collections. You may have to take the materials away for this work; to avoid any misunderstanding, give the landowner a receipt. The receipt should state the number and types of artifacts and the conditions under which you are permitted to retain them.

A landowner who trusts and respects the integrity of the archaeologist is an important asset to any project. It is the job of everyone on the excavation to do everything possible to establish and maintain this trust, on behalf of the project, the dig director and the sponsors of the work.

If the name of the owner or tenant of a piece of land is not known, you can usually get it from the land registry office records, or by spending an hour or so in the nearest community talking with various officials. The local postmaster, municipal township or county clerks, foremen of local road maintenance crews, local newspaper reporters or editors, or the nearest general store are useful places to check on local land-owners. A visit to the house nearest a site may be all that is necessary to identify the ownership of a parcel of land. The whole process, like most of the work of field surveying, will require time and patience.

The basic equipment for a field survey includes a clip-board with a smooth surface, a supply of paper (both plain and graph) for sketches, field survey record forms, mechanical pencils with 2H to 4H lead and pocket pointer, pocket pencil sharpener, eraser, a topographic map of 1:50,000 or 1:25,000 scale or larger, a 35mm camera with film for black and white and coloured photos, polyethylene and paper bags, tape for sealing bags, a bricklayer's pointing trowel with a 5-inch or smaller blade, a 10-metre long cloth tape, and if necessary a hard hat. Most of this equipment can be carried in a rucksack or an airline bag with a shoulder strap.

If you can carry more, a second camera is recommended, so that you can use one for black and white photographs and the other for coloured slides. Personal equipment will depend on the terrain, and may include stout boots, mosquito or black-fly spray, a sun-hat, and a small first-aid kit. Finally, it is always advisable to have a companion along on all field survey work. This will reduce the time required and provide help in any accident.

LOCATING SITES

There are a number of aids to locating a site on the ground. Some of these have been introduced in the previous chapter, under documentary sources, and include early maps, maps in county atlases, deed descriptions, etc. These sources may locate the site on a particular lot and concession, but they will not give its precise location or the extent of features on the lot. Knowing the more recent uses of a piece of land may give you important information about the fate of an historic site. For example, the search for the Foster Brothers Glass Works of Port Colborne, Ontario continued to frustrate field survey workers, who knew the lot and concession of the works but were unable to find any remains. Investigation of the activities of a nearby limestone

quarry finally showed that the extension of quarrying onto the site of the glass works had destroyed all traces of it. There is always the possibility that early records do not give the full extent of land use: for example, the full dimensions of a quarry or brick yard. Many industries expanded beyond the limits documented; only by actual field observations can these limits be determined accurately.

Useful aids to field survey work include maps, aerial photographs, probes and augers, and observations of crop marks and surface artifacts. Recently, geophysical prospecting devices have been applied to archaeological problems, providing more sensitive means of delineating the extent of an historic site.

Maps

Workers should be familiar with the use of modern large-scale maps, essential to all field surveying. A wide range of them exist, although maps of less populated parts of the country may be hard to find. There are the town maps and street directories or guidebook maps sold at news-stands and stationers, and the maps available from municipal, township or regional engineering and planning offices, from land developers, and from provincial government offices. You can usually get large-scale maps free from local government offices, or for a nominal price; these can be used as base maps for sketch plans (see figure 4.1) or, later, in preparing site maps for publication (see chapter 10). Larger public libraries, universities with map collections in either their library or geography department, or provincial departments dealing with municipal matters such as the departments of highways or natural resources may have maps you will find useful.

The basic maps for all field survey work are the National Topographic System maps, available from the Canada Map Office, Department of Energy, Mines and Resources, 615 Booth Street, Ottawa K1A 0E9. They cover all of Canada but the larger scaled maps, which are most useful for field survey work, (1:25,000) are available only for the more densely-populated areas. Unlike many of the local maps which deal primarily with roads, hydro lines and property lines, the

Figure 4.2. Section of a topographic map of Grimsby, Ontario at a scale of 1:25,000. Courtesy Dept. of Energy, Mines and Resources, Ottawa

Figure 4.3. Same area as figure 4.2 but at a scale of 1:50,000 giving less detail than the 1:25,000 scale but a greater area of land surface. Courtesy Dept. of Energy, Mines and Resources, Ottawa

1:25,000 scale map will give a good indication of the churches and settlements which may have since disappeared. The date of the map's latest revision, printed in the margin, will give you the date after which changes in land use have not been recorded. More recent aerial photographs may help to update a topographic map.

1:25,000, approximately 2.5 inches on the map representing 1 mile on the ground, is the largest scale used by the National Topographic system. This scale is large enough to give a good indication of the terrain, modern municipal boundaries, and an accurate representation of the shape of larger buildings. The location and extent of quarries, brickyards, railroad yards, and hydro and communications lines, information useful for field work involving industrial sites, are also shown. The location of cemeteries on maps may also provide a clue to archaeological sites, as cemeteries were often beside or near now vanished churches and settlements.

The 1:50,000 scale series, roughly 1.25 inches on the map representing 1 mile on the ground, is the commonest field survey map. This series is available for all the major settled areas of Canada and shows sufficient details for most field survey work.

Indexes to all maps of the 1:50,000 scale series as well as lists of other maps produced by the Federal government can be obtained free from the Canada Map Office, Ottawa. A complete catalogue of published maps, including topographic maps, photomaps, thematic maps and atlases can be obtained from these sources. Good introductory guide to topographic map use are *Every Square Inch*, by L.M. Sebert and *Everyone Should Be Able To Use a Map*, both available from the Canada Map Office or Information Canada.

Aerial Photographs

Rapid change in land-use is particularly important to you as a field worker in historical archaeology, because many of the important sites are near or influenced by centres of rapid growth. Aerial photographs provide a wealth of surface information. They are available for all of Canada and include virtually every site of potential interest to the historical archaeologist. In the National Air Photo Library in Ottawa is an index of over four million aerial photographs of varying scales, taken during the last half-century. In addition to black and white photographs, colour photographs are available of some areas. All are available on microfilm; by consulting an index map showing the relative ground position of the photography, the photograph of a particular area can be obtained rapidly. Provincial ministries of national resources also have collections of aerial photographs, of varying scale, from which you can get contact prints at nominal cost.

The best way to obtain aerial photographs is to mark the area of interest on a topographical (1:50,000) map and send the map, together with a description of the tract(s) of land desired, to the National Air Photo Library of the provincial government air photo library. State whether you want the latest photograph or the one with the largest scale. The commonest scale is 1:2,000 or 1:3,000, but for a slightly higher cost you can get enlargements up to five times the original size (9x9 inches). Remember that as the scale increases the ground area that can be represented is reduced.

If a suitable recent aerial photograph is not available, you may be able to obtain one from a commercial aerial photography company or to arrange for a member of a local flying club to do the work for you. These services can be very expensive, though.

The currently available aerial photographs of Canada have not been taken specifically for archaeological purposes, but for mapping and analysis of the landscape. The two principal types are the oblique and the vertical. Oblique photographs are taken from an airplane with the camera held at an angle less than 90 degrees to the earth. Vertical photographs are taken, as the name suggests, straight down, and are useful in making site and regional plans. The stereoscopic study of air photographs allows three-dimensional views of the earth as it appears from above, providing realistic proportions for the various surface features. Introductory books on aerial photography describe the use of the stereoscope and how to interpret stereograms.

You may want to locate early aerial photo-

Plate 4.1. Aerial photograph of David Burns Pottery site (arrow). Courtesy Ontario Ministry of Natural Resources

graphs of a particular site for comparison with more recent ones, to evaluate the changes that may have occurred.

Probe Bar and Auger Surveys

Where time limitations make it necessary to locate the features of a site as quickly as possible, a probe bar or auger survey may be the best. You can make a probe bar by welding a 3- to 4-foot pointed steel bar 0.5 or 0.625 inches in diameter to a short steel handle to create a T shape. The probe is forced into the ground at fixed spaces across a site and the relative position of walls or other structures determined by the resistance encountered. A probe bar survey works best where the underground features are different

from the earth that surrounds them. Probing a site completely covered with brick or rock, for instance, will not give you any precise information on the location of the remains of brick or stone walls below.

On the minus side, a probe bar survey is very hard work, gives imprecise results, and may damage important artifacts beneath the surface.

A soil auger, of which a post-hole digger is one form, has a T-bar or handle equipped with an auger or boring device. The auger is screwed into the ground, and the soil and other materials picked up are retrieved for examination when the auger is extracted. Soil augers are used extensively by soil scientists and can be obtained from scientific supply houses or made for a survey team by a local welding shop. They have, however, the same drawbacks as probe bars.

Visual Observations

You will of course look carefully at the growth of crops or grass over a site, the appearance of any features, contour changes, and any artifacts. Walls or other features under the soil may affect the growth of grass or crops above. Where these features are just under the soil surface, they may limit the depth of soil for plants, thereby altering the amount of moisture available. During a dry spell one patch of crops or grass may turn comparatively browner or yellower, and so indicate the outlines of walls or other features. These brown areas may be quite pronounced if observed at the right time during the dry season.

Not all brown areas on a site will be attributable to a buried feature, as geological or other factors may also influence drainage patterns and thus plant growth. In addition, important features may not noticeably affect the surface vegetation at all. For these reasons crop or sod marks should be combined with other information when assessing the visual evidence on a site.

Artifacts such as pot sherds are virtually indestructible and are a positive clue to the location of a settlement or a pottery works. Likewise, brick debris and concentrations of glass, iron fragments, coins, or buttons may indicate the location of a house or other feature. You should notice the pattern of distribution of the surface artifacts as well as the variety of material. This is especially important where surface depressions may indicate the location of a former house, well or auxiliary building. Since building and other human activity frequently involve use of landfill and levelling, any change in what appear to be the natural contours of the site should be carefully noted.

Resistivity Surveying

In recent years a number of new scientific aids have been employed in site survey work. These devices have been used in the physical sciences, particularly in geophysics and geology, and have been adapted to archaeology. Unfortunately, excavators with limited funds will find it difficult to obtain the use of these instruments unless the excavations are undertaken with the aid of a museum or university that has the equipment. In Canada the most useful device is the resistivity meter. Electromagnetic instruments and the proton-magnetometer are also used for site survey work, but these are very specialized instruments and go beyond the scope of all but the most sophisticated historical excavations. Further information on the latter instruments can be found in any of the standard reference works on field archaeology listed in the Bibliography.

The resistivity survey determines patterns of electrical resistance beneath the surface of the ground. When water is present in the spaces between rocks and soil particles it frequently contains dissolved mineral salts and forms a good conductor of electrical current. Consequently, the amount of electrical resistance offered by soil and rock layers will vary with the amount of moisture present, and the porosity of the soil itself. Ordinary soil, which normally has a large number of very small moisture-holding passages, has a lower electrical resistance than the denser bedrock on which it rests, assuming there is not a high water table. Likewise, loose soil with large air spaces will hold very little moisture and will provide locally higher resistance to an electrical current. This does not mean that all variations will necessarily indicate a disturbance of archaeological significance, as the

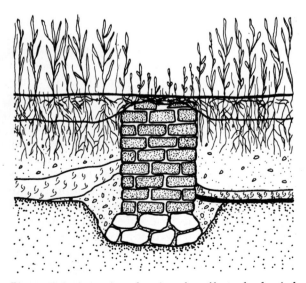

Figure 4.4. A section showing the effect of a buried structure on the growth of plants.

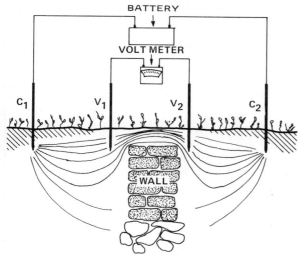

Figure 4.5. An electrical current flowing from probe C_1 to C_2 is interrupted by an architectural feature, causing the voltmeter attached to rods V_1 and V_2 to register a change in current caused by the feature.

soil itself will have local variations due to normal geological processes. The detection of features of archaeological significance is possible, however, because human disturbances have a regular pattern that can be detected in the interpretation of the resistivity survey results.

Resistivity measurements are made by inserting four metal spikes (electrodes) in the ground generally in a straight line, each connected by an insulated wire to a battery-operated resistivity meter. The resistance of the ground is found by introducing an electrical current into the ground, usually through the two outer electrodes, and simultaneously measuring the potential difference (i.e. voltage) between the other two electrodes. The instrument gives readings of resistance, expressed in ohms, that indicate the average resistance of a volume of ground centred around the mid-point of the line of electrodes.

To conduct a resistivity survey stretch a cloth tape across a site and insert the probes at equal spaces, beginning at one end of the traverse. By plotting the values of the resistance on a graph, with the distance as the abscissa and the readings in ohm-feet as the ordinate, you can plot a curve indicating anomalies.

The spacing of electrodes will determine the depth to which the current will flow. Generally speaking, the rule is that the distance between electrodes will equal the depth of detection. In archaeological work the spacing between electrodes and the depth of the electrodes in the ground is kept constant as a series of readings are taken across a site. This will measure the average resistance to a constant depth. Figure 4.6 shows the results of a resistivity survey at Fort York, Toronto, measured along a traverse set at right angles to the length of the site of the early log barracks. The distance between anomalies on the curve approximates the distance between walls of the barrack buildings shown on early plans of the Fort. The graph gives the excavators an indication of where to lay out their squares and the possible extent of the features of a site.

THE SITE SURVEY FORM

Organizations and individuals sponsoring field survey work should develop a form comprehensive in scope yet manageable and flexible enough to bring together various kinds of information. The exact format of a survey form will depend on the number of sites to be visited and the purpose of the survey. If your survey involves hundreds of sites you will need an efficient method of cataloguing the information on the forms; if it is more limited you may find it convenient to use a form already available from a museum or university archaeology or anthropology department.

Completed survey forms should be deposited in a central location, such as a museum, local library, or public archives, where they will be available on agreed terms for public use. Each field survey form should be stored in a site document file which should also include other relevant historical documentation, plans of any existing structures, a site sketch, photographs, a list of surface artifacts collected, and the location where these artifacts are stored. The results of field surveys should be reported in local archaeological or historical journals, especially if further work is impossible. If a site has been destroyed, a published report should note this,

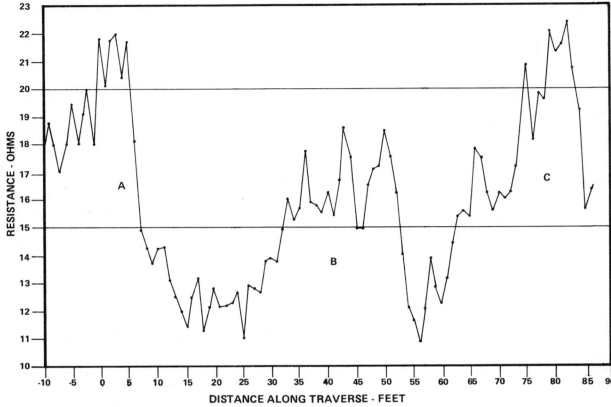

Figure 4.6. Resistivity curve at Fort York indicating three high anomalies which might indicate three underground features, shown by high resistance.

to save others the effort involved in searching for it.

A typical field survey form in use at the Canadiana Department of the Royal Ontario Museum, Toronto, is shown in plate 4.2. The following are some of the categories of information you should record.

TYPE OF SITE AND MAP LOCATION

Field survey records are filed at the Royal Ontario Museum according to the type of site and its map location. The site may be domestic, military, or industrial. Each of these categories can be further subdivided according to the needs of the field survey work. For example, the industrial sites could be classified as pottery, grist mill, iron foundry, or glass factory, to name a few possibilities.

Recording location according to the military grid reference used on all 1:25,000 and 1:50,000 NTS maps provides a standard, Canada-wide means of precisely locating any site. The entire country is divided into 100-kilometre squares, each of which is identified by two uppercase letters. Each 100-kilometre square is further subdivided into kilometre squares. Any point on the map can be represented by the two upper case letters and a six-digit number, the first three digits of which represent the distance of the site east of the western boundary of the kilometre square in which the site is located; the second set of three digits represents its location north of the southern boundary. The first two numbers of each set of three digits refer to the particular kilometre square, while the third number represents the tenths of a kilometre east or north within the kilometre square. The military grid reference will therefore locate a site correctly to the nearest 100 metres.

SITE SURVEY

1. Site Name __Huron Pottery__
2. Address __Egmondville__
3. County __Huron__ Township __Tuckersmith__
4. (Country)/City/Province __Egmondville, Ontario__
5. Location details __the pottery is located on Lot 3 on the north side of Stanley Street. The street is now a grand County road beginning immediately north of the bridge over the Bayfield River.__

   __MU 670205__
   GRID REF.
   __industrial (pottery)__
   TYPE OF SITE

6. Historical dates for site __1852 - 1910__
7. Present Owner: Name __Mr. & Mrs. William Huggett__
   Address __Egmondville, P.O.__   Tel. No. __527-0987__
8. Present Tenant (if applicable): Name __none__
   Address ___-___   Tel. No. ___-___
9. Owner's Attitude to archaeological work __The owners are interested in further archaeological exploration by a qualified research team. They indicate they would cooperate with such work.__
10. Attitude of tenant (if applicable) ___/___

11. Informants:

Name	Address	Tel. No.
Mr. William Hart	Seaforth, Ontario	527-1972
Mr. Harry Thompson	RR 2, Clinton, Ontario	-
Mrs. Claire Pretty	Goderich St., Seaforth	-

SITE SURVEY FORM   -2-

12. Description of site (including buildings) __The site indicates the probable location of the pottery kiln and pottery cellar by a careful study of the depressions in the surface. The borders of these knolls on the west and north may also indicate the extent of the pottery building. A known trait in 1930's across the waste dumps (seen in regard 'cut' not near a barn). A 'ramp' may indicate location of distribution debris of kiln.__

13. Possibility of site destruction __The owners plan to build a garage on the site sometime after 1976 and it is recommended that archaeological work be conducted before that time.__

14. Nearest source of water (excluding wells) __No farm water. A stream to the north of site is usual in the summer.__

15. Vegetation __The site is covered with spruce, apple and walnut trees except immediately along roadside.__

16. Soil on site __Clay-loam__

17. Possibility of cultivation __The site is presently a lawn and there is no prospect of it being changed.__

18. Erosion __There is no evidence of erosion at the site.__

19. Record of disturbances __Several small holes indicate that 'pot-hunters' have been busy at the site within the past five to six years. These disturbances are not so extensive as to have destroyed major parts of the site.__

20. Published historical and archaeological references __References to the pottery: Valentine Bohler (1852-1876), Jacob Wehn (1876-__

Plate 4.2. A completed survey form.

SITE SURVEY FORM -3-

1897), Joseph Weber (1897-1900), J. Allan (1900) & Ferdinand Burgard (1900-1910) are found in county and provincial directories; Mercantile Agency Reference Books, and local history works. Both Shackleton's Pottery list for Ontario and Collard's pottery book list known references to site. There have been no archaeological reports published on the site as of this date.

21. Site sketch map (include physical features and contours)
ATTACH AS SEPARATE SHEET

22. Photographs of site (colour, black & white)

1:1 Overall view of site from the south b&w
1:2 View of possible remains of kiln, from south b&w
1:3 Evidence for the remains of walls of pottery building, photo taken from the east b&w
1:4 The waster dump behind the modern barn, photo taken from the north, facing south b&w
1:5 Fragment of cream pot found on surface, colour

23. Surface artifacts collected
SEE SHEET 4

24. Recorded by Dhewlands Date June 29, 1974

SITE SURVEY FORM -4-

23. SURFACE ARTIFACTS COLLECTED

Museum mark on artifacts EG 74

Registration Number	Description
EG 74-1	rim of cream pot, rim dia. 24cms.; sherd glazed yellow
EG 74-2	Wedge, 1.2 cm wide, 1.5cm long
EG 74-3	base of milk pan, glazed with rust-red speckled colour; glazed on both the inside and outside of vessel.
EG 74-4	medicine bottle, hand-blown, clear glass; bottle 10cms. high, circular, with 5cm. diameter
EG 74-5	rim of mixing bowl; rim dia. 25cms.; rim glazed yellow colour
EG 74-6	rim of preserve jar; 10 cms. dia.; glazed yellow colour on both inside and outside of jar.
EG 74-7	'body' sherd; glazed yellow on inside and outside.
EG 74-8	fragment of a 'strap' handle from a butter crock. Fragment glazed yellow colour on outside.
EG 74-9	base of flower pot; dia. at bottom 12cm.; unglazed

Plate 4.2. continued

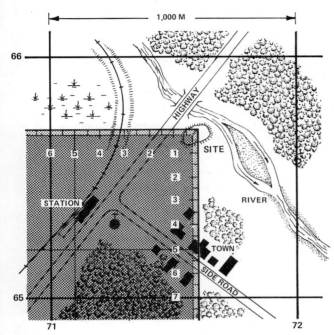

Figure 4.7. Determining the location of a land mark within a 1 km square with the use of a romer. (Site location is 716657).

A further description of the location of the site can be entered on the survey form. You should describe the lot and concession number and other details of a site that relate to modern roads, existing buildings or natural features. When a site is outside the limits of a town, borough or city, use the name and number of the nearest public road. Remember to write your description in a form that will enable another researcher to locate the site easily.

SITE NAME, ADDRESS, HISTORICAL DATES

The site may be known by the name given by the owners or their predecessors, or it may have the name of the business that operated there. Report the postal address for a site, but make sure that the postal address is the same as the name of the municipality in which the site is located. The dates between which the site was occupied by the house, fort or industry that is the subject of the survey should be included, if you know them.

OWNER AND TENANT RECORD

The name, address and telephone number of the owner or tenant should be recorded, with a brief assessment of his attitude toward the preservation of the site for future archaeological work.

INFORMATION FROM LOCAL INDIVIDUALS

In any field survey there are usually people other than the owner or tenant who have information pertaining to the site. These individuals should be interviewed, their comments recorded, and the information included in the site document file.

DESCRIPTION OF THE SITE

A complete description of the physical features of the site, including the area of occupation and the present structures, should be recorded. If it is possible to measure the structures, include a scaled plan in the report.

POSSIBILITY OF SITE DESTRUCTION

Record any information from the owner or other individuals concerning possible changes in land use that would threaten the existence of the site. Any threat to the site may influence the timing of further field work.

VEGETATION, WATER, SOIL TYPE AND OTHER GEOGRAPHICAL FEATURES

Describe the type of vegetation on the site, the location of the nearest source of water, the type of soil and the effects of erosion, and the possibility of the site being cultivated during the time of projected field excavations.

RECORD OF DISTURBANCES

All previous archaeological excavation at the site should be described, as well as the extent of any destruction caused by new roads or road regrading, housing, farming, or other causes. You may not observe some disturbances without walking carefully over the site several times. The local or provincial highway departments may have survey plans or other records to indicate the changes made for road-work. (Copies of any other published archaeological reports on the site should be filed with the site survey report.)

THE SITE SKETCH PLAN

Make a sketch plan showing all the natural and man-made features of a site, including existing buildings, roads, field boundaries, and the location of any observable remains of archaeological significance. A sketch plan can be completed in a short time, and if done carefully can be used in publications about the site. You will need a clipboard with a smooth surface, a supply of 8.5 x 11-inch graph paper, a pencil (2H to 4H), a straight-edge, and an eraser.

By walking around the prominent features of a site and looking at them from all angles, you can plot their relative sizes and relationships to one another. Distances between features and their individual dimensions can be approximated using a measured pace. When the main features have been drawn, the secondary features, such as fence lines, walkways, etc., are added as accurately as possible. Notes to indicate the identification of buildings, the use of fields, the condition of roads, and the importance of archaeological remains should be made on the sketch plan. It should be labelled: *Not to Scale— Sketch Plan.*

If a 1:25,000 or 1:50,000 NTS topographic map of the area is available, you can use it as a guide to locating the larger features of the site. Each feature of the sketch plan should be seen as part of the larger site, and located on the plan at its relative distance from other features.

One of the best ways to show changes in the land surface is the use of *hachures*, a system of symbols used for many centuries on English ordinance survey maps. The hachure looks like a tadpole with the head at the top of the slope and the tail pointing downhill. The heavier the hachure the more important the feature at a site. The shape of the head varies according to changes or breaks of slope: a rounded head indicates a gradual change of slope and a flat-topped head a sharply-defined break. Close together, hachures indicate a steep slope; farther apart they indicate a more gentle one. The length of the tail of the hachure is related to the length of the slope. The tail always points downhill.

Hachures should be used only for man-made features and not contours and other natural features of a site.

If you have time for a more detailed site sketch and if such a sketch would help in the evaluation of a site, make a contour survey. To make a contour survey, place a base line along the length of the site. At measured distances of 1, 2, or 5 metres along this base line, set perpendicular lines extending across the width of the site with twine anchored by stakes or nails. A dumpy level (see Glossary, and chapter 7 for details

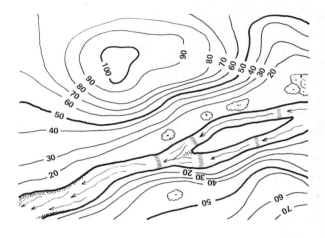

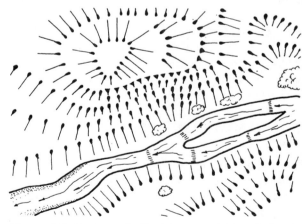

Figure 4.8. Contours indicate an area of equal elevation; a group of contours of different elevation indicate either a hill or depression. Contour lines are based on exact measurements. Hachures also indicate hills or depressions but are done without detailed measurements.

on the use of the level) is used to determine the elevations of points at established intervals (usually 1 metre), along these lines, and the reduced level for each point is located on a scale plan laid out on graph paper. Areas of similar height are joined to form contour lines.

PHOTOGRAPHS

Record the general site layout and all important features in both black and white and colour photographs. Note the subject of each picture, the direction of the photograph and a description of the prominent features. A metric scale should be placed in the photographs whenever possible to give a reference for measurement of all features. Further details on photography are discussed in chapter 8.

SURFACE COLLECTIONS

Collect any artifacts you find on the ground during the field survey. Typical artifacts are fragments of pottery, glass, metal, clay pipe stems, window glass, buttons, coins and marked bricks. A list of the artifacts indicating the identity of each should be included in the survey report. If time permits it would be useful to define the areas within the site perimeter where each type came from. This may aid future excavation and help determine where to dig. As well as the quantity of artifacts you find, note any detail, such as the shape of a pot, that might indicate

function. You should also state the method used to register artifacts, and their place of deposit. Various samples such as soil, wood, metal and slag may also be collected.

NAME OF RECORDER AND DATE OF SURVEY

The field worker should sign and date all survey forms. When a number of workers participate, the name of the person who verifies or checks the information on the forms before they are filed should be recorded. If copies of a survey report are sent to other institutions or individuals, record any exchange in the field survey form, together with the date of transmission. This information is important in cases where full public disclosure of the contents of a survey might result in plundering or wanton destruction of a site by treasure-hunters.

Evaluating The Field Survey

One does not excavate a site simply because it is there. Excavations should add significant information to what is already known, or shed light on the over-all regional context of which the site is only one element. These days the rate of destruction is far greater than the resources available for excavation. The archaeologist, in consultation with scientists from related disciplines, must be ready to assess each site survey report to determine whether the results of excavation could justify the time, work, and money demanded.

Chapter 5

PREPARING FOR THE EXCAVATION

Before beginning to dig you must get permission from both the provincial government and the owner of the property you plan to excavate. The legislation controlling archaeological activities in each province is found in the Appendix. In Ontario, all field surveys and excavations in the Province must be licensed under section 48 of the Ontario Heritage Act of 1974. The questions asked of the applicant for a license under this Act can be used as a guide to the information that most Canadian provinces require from a prospective excavator. Applicants must state the nature and purpose of the project, the relevant academic and field experience of all staff members, the methods and procedures planned for the recovery, dating, cataloguing, conservation and restoration of artifacts, the project's financial and material resources, the place of disposition of archaeological objects and records, and the plans for publication. The government may also require written proof of the land-owner's consent to the work. A government license does not imply that the recipient has the right to trespass or in any way usurp the rights of private property.

Before applying for a license, walk over the site with the owner and discuss the proposed dig, its purpose, its timing and the anticipated size of the crew. Once you have come to an agreement, get the owner's written consent, especially in provinces where it is necessary for a license to excavate. This statement should define the area to be excavated, and the access routes that the diggers will use each day. You may also want to know the landowner's wishes about visitors walking over his land.

The landowner should know and agree to the length of time that the dig will take. The ownership and disposition of all artifacts is also an important item, to be clearly stated in the written agreement. Artifacts should be deposited in a public institution that has an active interest in historical archaeology, although the person who is to publish the excavation report normally has the right to use the artifacts until the report is finished. Resist any agreement by which the landowner, a private individual or an organization with little or no interest in historical archaeology obtains final possession of artifacts: your objective as an archaeological field worker is to uncover information that will be available to everyone.

An agreement between the sponsors of the excavation and the landowner should also state who has the right to publish the results of the dig, the kind and amount of insurance to be carried by the sponsor of the field work, where excavated earth is to be dumped, and how the site is to be filled and left after the work is completed. If the landowner or the owner of a nearby house is willing to provide hydro, water, telephone and a mailing address then an agreement on payment for these services should also be made before the dig begins.

Finally, it is a courtesy to the landowner to provide a list of the names and addresses of the people who will be working on his land. This can be a practical advantage as the landowner may be able to forward mail and receive telephone messages for known members of the dig.

FINANCES

Most excavations have a limited budget; large sums of money for archaeological work are usually available only to educational institutions and government agencies. For local digs you will probably have to appeal to community service clubs, local historical societies, and municipal or county councils. Private individuals may donate small sums. Remember that you may be able to register a dig or its sponsors as a Canadian charitable organization. You can then issue receipts valid in calculating income tax deductions. A sympathetic public may also donate supplies, services, food, and other items.

A dig budget should allow for food, lodging, rental of laboratory and storage space, hydro, telephone, photography, conservation, and other technical department supplies, costs associated with travel to and from the dig, insurance, and the cost of replacing sod or other covering of the ground at the end of the dig. There should also be a supplementary item for the cost of preparing the final excavation report. This will amount to 20 to 40 per cent of the cost of the field work. Your budget must reflect the actual cost of the field work; an unrealistic budget will mean a shortage of funds during the dig, which can lead to undesirable shortcuts in the excavation methods. The full cost of the project should be raised before the field work is begun. Include a "miscellaneous" item for small unexpected costs.

A dig in May of 1974 at a western Ontario pottery site with twenty volunteers who worked a month cost approximately $200 per volunteer for the duration of the work. This sum included the cost of replacing supplies used in the work, but did not include the initial cost of equipment. If staff members are paid a salary then the budget will have to be increased significantly.

STAFF AND ORGANIZATION

The excavation of an historical site usually involves a small crew, from six to twenty-five workers. The size of the crew will be determined by the nature and extent of the dig, its length, and the money available. A small Ontario industrial site in the centre of a village may require

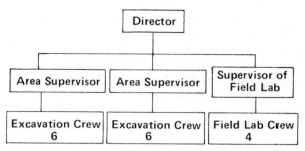

Figure 5.1. Staff organization pyramid.

only six staff members for a month; excavation at a large military fort may call for twenty or more. A staff of twenty, composed of two excavation crews and one field laboratory crew, might be structured as shown in figure 5.1. This staff could be reduced to sixteen if the director doubles as the supervisor of the field laboratory and each of the three supervisors also work as members of their respective crews. There are a number of possible staff structures, but whatever organization you develop, stick to it, to avoid confusion and conflict among the workers. The smaller the staff the closer the personal relationships, and the more versatile and flexible each member must be. A larger staff means a greater chance for specialization although even then everyone must be prepared to do the jobs he expects others to do.

All digs need as many experienced and qualified archaeologists as possible. It is not always possible to have a complete staff of experienced diggers, but some should be available to assist and direct the novices. A completely inexperienced staff is a drain on the director and area supervisors and slows down the digging.

Wages for diggers are increasingly common. One reason for this is that universities and government departments must compete for workers on the summer student labour market, and have the resources to do so. This precedent of paying competitive wages is making it difficult for a local organization to sponsor a dig on a small budget. Yet the future of historical archaeology lies in these local groups developing trained and competent teams able to work effectively in their own areas. If the trend towards wages continues, there will be more and more pressure on governments to provide more and more money for archaeology.

There is an alternative approach. On several digs the authors have successfully used volunteers only, covering their travel expenses to and from the site, and all living expenses, including accident insurance. There is a wider range of ages among volunteers than among paid students; one summer's crew consisted of a government short-wave radio-operator, a high school student, a public school teacher, a university student of anthropology, and two housewives. Some were on vacation, other had left their jobs and volunteered in order to learn about field work. Various other interested individuals turned up on weekends. Needless to say the team proved very enthusiastic, working from early morning to after nine in the evening with only short breaks for meals and tea.

Most excavation crews consist of a director, one or more area supervisors, excavation crew members, a supervisor of the field laboratory, and a field laboratory crew.

Director

The director is in charge. He is responsible for everything done during the field excavations and ultimately for the quality and archaeological value of the information produced. He, therefore, must be experienced in field excavation and trained in all aspects of historical archaeology, from preliminary research techniques to preparing the results of the dig for publication. This training may have been acquired "through the ranks" as a field worker, or formally.

The director must know how to do all the jobs involved in a dig. He determines the techniques that will be used in the excavation, and the overall day-to-day application of these techniques to the field work. He usually plans the daily work with the area supervisors, to whom he delegates the responsibilities of excavation of each area of the site.

The director's ability to delegate authority to area supervisors and the technical staff, and to earn the respect and confidence of all the workers, are crucial to his leadership. Certain responsibilities, once delegated, are difficult to retrieve, and so it is important that the director know what tasks to delegate, and to whom.

One responsibility that only the director should handle is public relations. Digs are often near built-up areas, and it is difficult to avoid attracting the curious as well as the keenly interested. The director should work out some arrangement for visitors. This will require the consent and cooperation of the landowner, and possibly that of the surrounding property owners. You may want to prepare a hand-out to explain the dig and the restrictions imposed on visiting it. Small wooden signs at strategic locations in the dig area can indicate areas closed to the public.

Invariably some enthusiast ignores polite requests and wanders all over the dig, sometimes leaning down to pull out an artifact from the soil. There is no ready prescription for handling this situation, but it should be the director who does it, not one of the volunteers.

The director should also handle contact with the press. The weekly community newspaper is an ideal vehicle for educating the public and for building good will towards the dig, and such papers are usually very cooperative. Nevertheless, they are apt to see archaeology as a form of entertainment. Archaeology is fun and should be, but fun is not its purpose. All reporters and photographers should be accompanied by the director, and discouraged strongly from taking "amusing" pictures of the dig - the kind that show two or three grinning heads peering over a wall. A release explaining the purpose of the dig and its major results may help the reporters understand why you are there.

When the excavation is finished, the director has the responsibility of planning and coordinating a report on the field work so that the information obtained is available to other archaeologists and the public at large. A director who does not plan to publish his results should not be doing field work in the first place. Excavating destroys most of the information available from a site; unpublished, it is lost forever.

Area Supervisor

The day-by-day decisions in the excavation of each area are made by its supervisor. He assigns each crew member his task for the day, and is responsible for instructing each crew member in the use of tools. An informal conference at a set time every day is a good way of ensuring that everyone is kept informed on progress and problems.

The area supervisor should have previous experience from a number of historical sites, and be able to oversee not only the digging, but also, if requested, photography, surveying, drawing, and the taking of samples in the area. He is the main link between the director and the excavation crew: through him the director's decisions are carried out. It is usual for the area supervisors and the director to plan each day's work together.

The area supervisor has the daily responsibility for completing the excavation record sheets, drawings of the vertical faces of the unexcavated earth (called the *baulks*) and all architectural features. He is responsible for labelling artifact buckets and baulk tags, and the collection and proper handling of delicate objects and samples.

Excavation Crew

The excavation crew is responsible for the digging of the site. Its members may be experienced or inexperienced and of varied ages and backgrounds. Ideally, there are six to a crew: three workers in the square, digging, trowelling, and gathering dirt into buckets; one bucket carrier and wheel-barrow pusher; and two sifters. Crew members usually have an opportunity to try each task. Some invariably find a certain task more to their liking and ask to do it permanently.

The diggers' tasks are the removal of soil by natural or occupational layers, the careful use of tools so that they do not destroy artifacts and soil evidence, the cutting of straight baulks, and the orderly collection of evidence. Workers should learn to clean the site continually while digging, to prevent loss or destruction of evidence and the contamination of one layer of artifacts by another. (This also reduces the time required for preparing the site for photography.) Since each area supervisor works closely with his excavation crew, the crew's application to these tasks is his responsibility. When he must be away from the dig, a well trained crew can continue on its own.

Field Laboratory Supervisor

Every excavation has a large and busy field laboratory. Here the data, artifacts, and samples that come from the diggings are processed and packed for shipment back to the permanent laboratory. The field laboratory also handles photography, conservation, and the taking of levels during the course of the excavation.

Supervising the field laboratory can be the most demanding job on a dig. Where the area supervisor may have but one area of four squares to attend to, the supervisor of the field laboratory is responsible for coordinating his crew to get several different tasks done properly at the same time.

Field Laboratory Crew

The typical field laboratory crew consists of five people, each one responsible for one of the following tasks: determining elevations of archaeological features and soil layers using a dumpy level or transit; taking photographs; maintaining registers of objects, elevations, artifact buckets and photographs; field conservation of artifacts recovered; and registering, bagging and boxing of artifacts and samples. On a small dig the supervisor of the field laboratory may do one or more of these jobs himself.

As the excavation crew removes layers of soil or architectural features, a member of the field laboratory crew and the area supervisor are needed to take elevations with a dumpy level or transit. The area supervisor should hold the rod, as only he will understand exactly where the level is to be taken and why. A complete photographic record of all layers and architectural features, in both black and white and colour, is essential for the published report on the dig. Black and white film may be processed on the site by the field laboratory worker responsible for photography. Remember not to remove features in a square until the black and white film has been processed and the results checked.

Four registers are maintained during an excavation: a register of all the artifact buckets

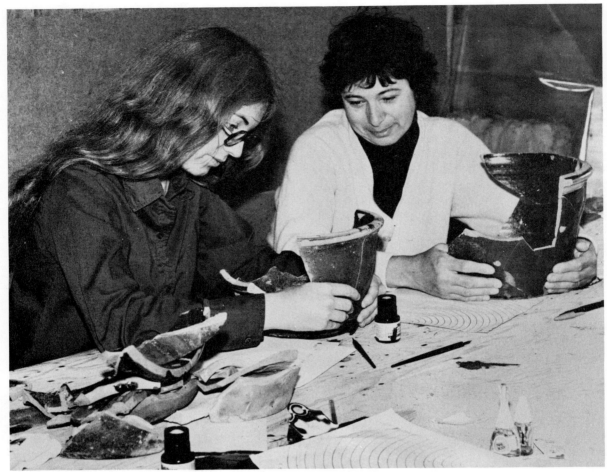

Plate 5.1. A field laboratory in operation at the David Burns Pottery Site, Holmesville, Ontario.

used in each square; a register of all the objects given specific numbers by the laboratory technicians; a register of all elevations; and a register of all black and white and coloured photographs taken on the site. The separate registers contain the information usually entered on the daily excavation record sheets. Separate registers make it easier to work with the archaeological data once the dig is over and the final report is being prepared. Further details about these registers will be given in succeeding chapters.

Working Conditions

Most digs operate at a minimum level of comfort and convenience. Few are equipped to handle volunteers with special physical restrictions, food requirements, or social preferences. Be sure your volunteers understand what the living conditions will be, but remember there is no automatic virtue in being uncomfortable. Few archaeologists expect to live in luxury, but primitiveness or bad planning masked as simplicity or ruggedness can lower morale on a dig faster than any other single factor.

In the summer crews usually prefer to begin work early in the morning, at 7:00 or 8:00 o'clock, and then take time off during the hottest hours for recreation, shopping, and visiting. After an early supper, they can resume work until dark. When making the daily schedule remember that field work demands more than banking hours; volunteers should expect to work long hours each day under what may be unusual conditions. At least a skeleton staff should be scheduled to remain on the site at all times.

Accident Insurance

Each worker should be covered by accident insurance on the site. This also protects the landowner, who may insist on such insurance before he gives permission to dig. Since all Canadian provinces have government-sponsored medical insurance plans, staff should be registered in one of these before the dig begins. A general physical examination and a tetanus inoculation are highly recommended as well.

EQUIPMENT

The type and amount of equipment necessary for an excavation depends largely on the site, the size of the staff, and the soil. Most historical sites can be excavated with a relatively simple set of tools you can buy from any good hardware store.

Individuals bring their own personal equipment to the site, and take responsibility for it. Excavation equipment is provided by the dig sponsors and is available each day from the technical department. Some directors ask diggers to bring their own trowels to the site, as this one piece of equipment more than any other is a matter of personal preference. A good trowel, tempered and seasoned, is a thing to cherish.

Personal Equipment

The basic dress requirement for digging is a set of old clothes that you don't mind getting dirty. A raincoat and rainhat, stout boots and a pair of running shoes, several pairs of socks, a warm sweater for evenings, and handkerchiefs come next. Workers should also bring towels, wash cloths, soap and shampoo, toiletries, and flatware and cutlery if required. A bathing suit is also a good idea.

Additional useful items are a pencil (HB, B or H), eraser, indelible black felt-tip pen, pen knife,

a small note pad, sunglasses, sunhat, an old pair of leather gloves (a good way for the beginner to avoid blisters), and a kneeling pad or small rubber mat. Experienced diggers find that a rucksack or a small airline shoulder bag is useful for carrying one's various accessories to the site, especially when living quarters are not located nearby.

Site Equipment

EQUIPMENT FOR THE EXCAVATION CREW

Each member of the crew should begin work with the necessary tools at hand. These include a 4-inch mason's pointing trowel, hand pick, hand broom, ½- and 2-inch wide paint brushes, hand shovel or dustpan, a 2-metre metal tape, a small ball of stout, non-stretching cotton twine, and a dozen common 3-inch nails. These tools can be brought to the site each morning in an empty bucket and returned in a bucket at the end of the day to the technical department.

Trowel

The only trowel to use is the flat mason's pointing trowel with the blade and tang in one piece. The less expensive kind with the blade riveted to the tang will last only a day or two before the blade and tang separate. The edges of the blade should be filed and kept sharp; whereas the point of the trowel should be rounded to reduce the chance of damaging artifacts as they are uncovered.

The trowel is used as a scraping tool, to remove one thin layer of soil at a time. To use, draw the blade towards you and place the dirt directly into the hand shovel or dustpan. A sharp eye will recognize artifacts lifted up with the dirt: remove these from the debris as it is loosened. When the hand shovel is full it should be dumped into a nearby bucket. If you use the trowel to gather soil into a pile, and then gather the pile of dirt into the hand shovel, you are doing twice as much work, while at the same time obscuring the soil layer underneath the dirt pile. Never use the trowel as a lever. When these tasks are to be done use a hand pick. As you draw the trowel towards yourself you gradually work forward to a predetermined objective. An experienced troweller should be able to remove thin layers of soil in a smooth and controlled manner, avoiding any unevenness.

Hand Pick

For more rapid excavation than is possible with a trowel, a small geologist's hand pick is used. The pick head should have one end pointed and the other flattened. Use the pick gently so that you can see at all times the effect of your blows. It should never be used so vigorously as to require a backswing. In confined areas a cavalier backswing of the pick may injure diggers working nearby.

In excavating a layer use the pick so that work progresses away from you, exposing a face of earth as the work continues. This procedure enables you to see the stratigraphy of the square as you remove soil.

Hand Broom

The hand broom is the basic cleaning tool. As the trowelling of a surface continues, the broom is used to remove loose soil and stones and to keep each unexcavated layer free from debris of the layer that is being excavated. If brooms are not available, a medium stiff bristle whisk is a suitable substitute. Use the hand broom with short, deliberate movements; energetic and wide-swinging movements scatter the dirt over the adjacent clean surfaces and may force your crew members to come the next day with goggles.

Paint Brushes

An assortment of inexpensive paint brushes are useful for removing soil from *in situ* objects, and cleaning of delicate features in preparation for photography.

Hand Shovel or Dustpan

The hand shovel, now a scarce item in hardware stores, has proved best for collecting debris. The shovel is placed on the ground and used as a scoop, with the debris pulled into it with a trowel and hand broom. When hand shovels are not available, use a durable metal or heavy-duty plastic dustpan instead. Thin plastic dustpans will last for one or two hours on the site before the weight of soil and stones breaks the handle from the blade.

Tapes, Twine and Nails

These are used for marking off special areas to control the limit of digging, and for the establishment of subsidiary baulks or probe trenches. Some diggers find it easier to dig by removing measured areas of a layer at a time, gradually extending the boundaries of the area to the whole square.

Buckets

You will need both plastic and metal buckets. When heavy or sharp stones or other debris are being moved, a metal bucket is better, since it will not be punctured when the material is dropped into it. Plastic buckets can be used for removing soil and light debris.

Other Equipment

The excavation crews will also share:

shovels (with rounded and squared blades)
spades
wheelbarrows
root-cutters (especially useful in removing tall weeds from a site)
hand pruning shears and grass-cutters
scythes
planking
rakes
sod cutting tool and/or square-bladed shovel
sledge hammer
hand sieves (0.25 and 0.5-inch mesh openings)
hand saw
chain saw
axe
polyethylene in sheets or rolls (.002 gauge)

The axe, hand saw, chain saw, sledge hammer, scythe, root-cutter, pruning and grass shears, sod cutting tool and rake will be needed at the beginning of the dig to prepare the ground for the grid or to remove brush and long grass. Shovels, spades, wheelbarrows, planking, buckets, hand sieves, and polyethylene are used during the course of the excavation, to remove the layers of soil from a square and to dump the debris in designated storage areas. The uses of these tools in the stages of excavation will be discussed in later chapters.

EQUIPMENT FOR THE AREA SUPERVISOR

The area supervisor will need a number of items in addition to those listed for the excavation crew. These items include two 20-metre cloth tapes, an 8-ounce plumb bob, a 2-metre metal tape or a 2-metre carpenter's rule, two line-levels, tags for artifact buckets and objects, a pound box of 2.5-inch common nails, 12-inch spikes for anchoring tapes, a clipboard with a smooth surface, graph paper, and a supply of the excavation record sheets. For handling artifacts and objects the area supervisor will need plastic bags, cardboard boxes, tags, elastic bands, twine and masking tape.

EQUIPMENT FOR THE FIELD LABORATORY

The field laboratory uses a wide assortment of equipment. Its extent and diversity will depend on the technical work done on the site and the personal preferences of the field laboratory crew. The items basic to the tasks of the technical department are listed below. The use of the equipment will be discussed in the sections dealing with each task.

Surveying, Levelling and Drawing of Plans and Sections

transit
dumpy level
plane table with legs
20-metre cloth tapes
2-metre metal tapes
metre-grid frame
18-inch wooden stakes
plumb bobs (8-ounce)
carpenter's spirit level
drawing board
pencil sharpener
pocket knife
Munsell colour charts
   (or standardized
   artist's paint colour
   samples)
calipers
set squares

surveyor's rod (metric)
metric pocket ruler
pencils — 2H - 4H
eraser (non-smudging)
non-stretching cotton string
6-inch nails

compasses
line levels
carpet tacks
roll of graph paper
elevation register forms
tracing paper
mechanical pencils and leads
   (2H to 4H)
pencil pointer
30-centimetre scales
T-squares

Equipment for Handling Artifacts and Objects

buckets (plastic and metal)
plastic bowls
dissecting needles
Incralac
paper boxes
packing material
masking tape
acetone
tarpaulins
folding chairs and tables
tent
ambroid adhesive

drying screens or egg cartons
india ink and pens
nail and tooth brushes
paper bags of various sizes
   from 1# to 20#
small plastic bags
tags
ball-point pens and felt-tip
   (indelible ink)
pencils — 2H
notebooks
masking tape (1 inch wide)
clip-board(s)

Photography

2 35mm cameras
lenses (28, 55 and
  135 mm)
tripod
film for cameras (b/w, colour)
dulling spray
garden hand sprayer or large
  atomizer
drawing board
level
dark cloth
photograph register forms

various metric scales for
  close work
filters
lens shield
step ladder (8-foot or 10-foot)
film changing bag
light meter
scaled sticks (5-, 10-, 25-,
  50-centimetre and 1-metre)
ball point pens (indelible
  ink)
pencils — H or 2H

Miscellaneous Equipment and Safety

A good first-aid box is essential for a dig, especially if there is no hospital close by. No dig known to the authors has not had a brisk demand for band-aids, surgical gauze and salt tablets. The first-aid box should be kept in an accessible place known to everyone, so that treatment can be administered without delay. A staff member trained in St. John ambulance first aid techniques could be placed in charge.

When squares are excavated to a depth of 50 centimetres or more, or work is conducted in wells or near the remains of high-standing walls, diggers should wear hard hats. Abide by the same regulations that construction companies are expected to follow concerning safety on the job. Contact the nearest provincial ministry of labour office to get them. All reinforcing of wells and walls should be checked by a government inspector before diggers are allowed to work in the area. There is no Canadian guide for safety standards on archaeological digs but the Council for British Archaeology, 7 Marylebone Road, London NW1 5HY England publishes a pamphlet called *Safety Precautions in Archaeological Excavations* that you should read.

Other useful items of equipment are ground sheets, a large thermos for each excavation crew, a portable propane stove, a large teapot, and a supply of good tea.

We have not tried to list equipment for feeding and lodging the staff. Guides to feeding large groups of campers are available, and whoever is responsible for organizing the field camp will want to make up his own list for this purpose.

A small trailer is a great morale booster during an arduous dig, as has been demonstrated to the authors during two successive seasons. Hot meals can be served from it, and the team can relax there after the day's work.

Sanitation

When a large staff has to be fed and housed in temporary quarters, adequate sanitation becomes an important item on the director's list of responsibilities. Standards for personal cleanliness and hygiene and for the handling of food, refuse and sewage must be maintained. On isolated sites, or digs located away from public sanitary facilities, it will be necessary to check the quality of drinking water and provide an acceptable method of disposing of refuse and sewage. (A handy and inexpensive guide is the *Sanitation Manual for Isolated Regions*, published by the Health Protection Branch of the Department of Health and Welfare.) Invite the local health officer or public health nurse to inspect your camp and advise you on proper health standards.

Chapter 6

BEGINNING THE EXCAVATION

Your first task in the excavation of a site is to remove all trees, shrubs, brambles and loose debris of twigs, small stones, and leaves in the squares to be dug. This initial cleaning will make work at the site easier, as well as help to keep the dig area clean as work progresses. A clean site is safer than a dirty one, as workers and wheelbarrows do not get entangled in brush and tree stumps.

A site that has been developed into a lawn is the least difficult to clean, as all it needs is a good mowing of the grass and a raking of the cuttings. Where uncultivated fields or woodlots are to be dug, more intensive preparations are necessary before the grid can be established. If tall trees and large bushes must be cut down, do so only after the landowner has given his permission. Trees outside the dig square may be kept, as their

Plate 6.1. The site is laid out with a string grid at an excavation that is about to begin.

shade makes digging more comfortable—and should the site become a tourist attraction they help to give it character. Cut trees and shrubs with a chain saw, small bushes and brambles with root cutters (loppers) and pruning shears. A final cleaning with a leaf rake will eliminate most of the remaining small twigs and dead leaves. Collect and label artifacts on the surface as described in chapter 9.

A good archaeologist was once defined as: "one who knows where to put dumps." There are many tales of dumps being placed on land later wanted for excavation. Store soil and debris from the squares as close to the worksite as possible, but where the piles will not contaminate the areas being dug, or be a prominent feature of site photographs.

If a site is on land normally cultivated or used as a garden, the different materials from the excavation should be put into separate dumps, i.e. the subsoil and larger stones placed in one location and the topsoil and sod in another. This will make it possible to replace the materials in the right order, so that the fertility of the land is not destroyed by the diggings.

ESTABLISHING A SITE GRID

The next step after cleaning is to establish a grid system over the site. A grid is a series of squares, marked by strings, that have been carefully surveyed or measured by hand. Each unit of the grid is assigned an identifying label. The purpose of the grid is to divide the site into smaller and more controllable units. You can then readily identify and document a given area of excavation and any artifacts and architectural features within it. The unexcavated units provide vertical sections showing layering of soil

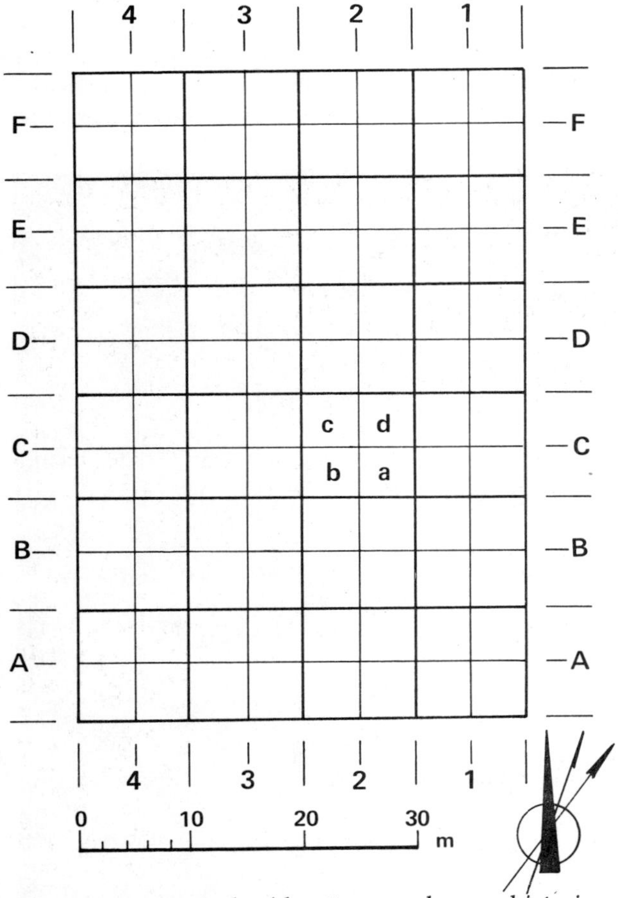

Figure 6.1a. Typical grid pattern used on an historical site.

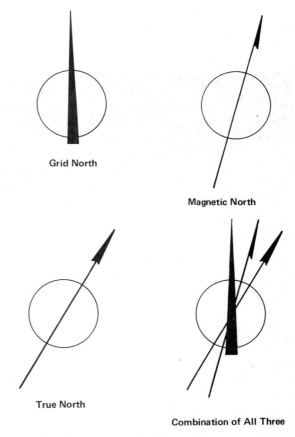

Figure 6.1b. Three types of north arrows and their combination.

and debris, as well as giving a means of transporting debris from the dig area to the dump.

The grid on an archaeological site is analogous to the grid of a road map. The area is divided into squares by lines going north to south and east to west. In an archaeological grid the space between two successive lines is called an *area.* Each area is divided into four *squares,* separated by four unexcavated vertical control units called *baulks.* An example of a grid on an Ontario site is shown in figure 6.1. A 10-metre interval was used, and each area divided into four 4-metre squares. The larger squares proved useful for the deep excavations at the site.

At Fort York, two areas in different parts of the fort were excavated at the same time by different crews. To coordinate the results of the dig and to avoid the confusion that would result if each site were gridded and labelled independently of the other, one master grid was established for the entire fort, and each site was dug as part of the larger grid.

Layout of the Grid

If there is a skilled surveyor on a dig staff, laying out the grid is a straightforward process, with the surveyor and an assistant using a transit and wooden stakes. Where there is no one with surveying skills or sophisticated surveying equipment available a few simple field procedures carefully followed will enable you to grid the site accurately.

If heavy equipment is to be used to remove a thick overburden, lay out the grid after this overburden is removed, otherwise the grid is removed with the overburden. And don't forget to take a lot of level readings all over the site, both before and after the overburden is removed. If this is not done it will be impossible to relate further elevations to the original sod line, which may be meaningful. A useful guide to the use of heavy equipment is the pamphlet, *Earthmoving on open Archaeological Sites,* by Francis Pryor.

ESTABLISHING THE GRID

Walk over the site and observe the relative sizes and shapes of buildings and natural features. You should take with you a copy of the site survey completed before the dig began. Comparing the survey and your own observations should help in forming a picture of the site. As you walk over the site, ask yourself questions, such as: "What is the most suitable location for the grid?" "What is the best size of grid interval?" "What will be the relationship of the grid to the architectural features to be excavated?" "Are there any special problems that might make it difficult to put a complete grid over the area?" "If so, what modifications should be made to the grid plan?" The grid should be located so that stakes will not have to be placed where they will not stay upright, on top of architectural features, or where they will be obscured by rocks or uneven ground.

The size and shape of the grid units will be influenced by the size of the site, the anticipated depth of the excavation, the nature of the soil, and the desired width of the baulks between squares. If you expect the excavation to be very deep or to go through loose rocks, sand, or other unstable materials, you will need larger grid units for the safety of the workers, facilitation of movement of debris to the surface, and photographing finds in the deeper parts of the square.

ORIENTING THE GRID

Orient your grid so that the squares are at an angle to any known walls. When walls are oriented in a north-south or an east-west direction, the grid should be established at a 45-degree angle to them to avoid any chance of the baulks covering undetected walls or other features.

ESTABLISHING THE BASE LINE

A base line is established along one edge of the site, as a reference for the grid that will be laid out against it. Use an 18-inch surveyor's stake to mark one end of the base line, setting the stake in the ground so that the sides are at a 45-degree angle with the grid. This will make the faces of the stake visible to diggers in the respective squares. Drive the stake into the ground with a sledge hammer, the deeper the better. Cut it off with a hand saw so that it will protrude about 5 or 6 inches above the ground surface. Spray the tops of the stakes with quick-drying orange paint; when this has dried place a carpet tack in the centre of the stake's top. Use a metric metal tape to locate the second stake of the base line the desired distance from the first. Place the second stake in the ground so that the line formed between the two tacks on the stakes forms the base line.

DETERMINING THE LOCATION OF GRID STAKES

Other grid stakes are located as follows. The base line is marked as A-B. If you can use a transit, then all that is necessary is to set the transit directly over the centre of the tack of stake A and to sight on the middle of the tack on stake B. Then locate the third corner stake C by turning the transit 90 degrees and indicating to your assistant the exact distance between A and C that should represent the desired length on the second axis of the grid area. Then reset the transit on stake C, backsight along A-C, and turn the transit 90 degrees to locate stake D. You can check the accuracy of the grid by sighting from D to A by turning the transit 45 degrees. The procedure can be repeated once more to check that the final sighting corresponds with stake B of the base line. If it does not, the angles of the grid are not 90 degrees and the work will have to be re-checked.

When the corner stakes have been placed, the transit can be re-set on stake A and the procedure repeated in order to locate all intermediate stakes.

Instead of using a transit you can establish the corners of the grid area by forming right-angled triangles at stakes A and B.

A right-angled triangle has its three sides in the ratio 3:4:5. Start at stake A and measure a distance of 3 metres along the base line toward stake B. Place a temporary stake (X) at this 3-metre point. Then attach a metric metal tape to stake A and a second tape to stake X. Place a second temporary stake (Y) where the distance of 4 metres on the tape A-Y intersects with the distance of 5 metres on the tape X-Y. Run a metal tape from stake A over the tack on stake Y to the desired distance to locate the corner stake C. Repeat this procedure at stake B to locate corner stake D. The positions of C and D can be checked

by measuring the distance between these stakes and by continuing the process of forming a right-angled triangle, now at stakes C and D.

The grid measurements are horizontal distances, not distances along the surface of the ground. If there is a downhill slope, measure the distances by holding the metric metal tape horizontal, using line levels if required, and using a plumb-bob on a string to locate the exact spot a stake is to be placed. In a high wind it is sometimes useful to use a 4-millimetre rod for the horizontal measurements, as it is not affected by the wind. Then lower the plumb-bob gradually until it is just above the ground. The midpoint of the swing of the plumb-bob is the point for the stake.

To measure a long horizontal distance on an uneven slope, you will have to make the measurements in stages. Figure 6.2 shows the method of plumbing across a depression. Extend a metal tape horizontally from position A a convenient distance (B), where a plumb-bob is used to locate a point (C) on the ground. A surveyor's arrow or an 8- or 12-inch wire nail is used to mark the point. Repeat this process at point C to measure the horizontal distance to D, remembering to keep the metal tape horizontal. A series of steplike measurements are made until the horizontal distance (A-J) across the slope has been measured.

Uphill measurements are made by following the same procedure up the slope. In figure 6.2, the horizontal distance G-H is measured by using a plumb-bob at F. This procedure can be repeated until the horizontal distance represented by the uphill slope has been measured.

When going across a depression or hill it is necessary to keep the horizontal measurements aligned with the grid axes. This can be done by using a series of ranging poles. Place two on the correct alignment and then sight along these two to place the third, fourth, etc. An alternative procedure is to use a compass to measure the angle of the grid string at the nearest stake (but keep the compass away from the metal tack). Sight along the string to the opposite side of the depression or hill.

Squares are marked with nails sunk into the ground. To determine the position of the corners of the squares, measure along and from the lines established for the areas. Sink the 12-inch nails

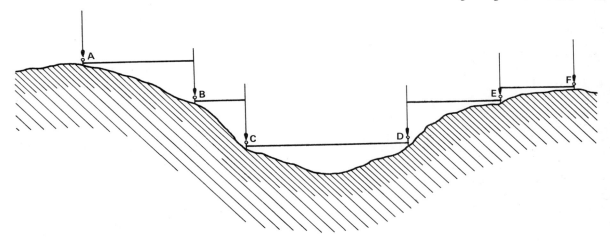

Figure 6.2. To plomb across a depression stretch a metal tape from point A to a second point where the tape is about chest height. Note the horizontal distance and by using the plomb bob and string locate a point B on the ground. Repeat this procedure for points C, D, E and F to complete the measurement. Add all distances to determine the distance from A to F.

into the ground until 1 inch or so remains visible, then stretch a continuous string along the perimeter of each square, wrapping it around each nail in turn. The nails can then be hammered flush with the ground surface. If a 12-inch nail cannot be sunk into the ground a smaller nail will have to be used, or the corners of the square will have to be off-set to a place where a nail can be secured to the ground.

Each square should be strung with a separate piece of twine to reduce the number of strings crossing the baulks. When each square is strung individually you can remove the string from one square without disturbing those of adjacent ones.

ESTABLISHING A TEMPORARY BENCH MARK

During the excavation all vertical measurements will be taken in reference to the top of a bench mark. Orange paint should be used to form a cross pattern for the bench mark. The intersection of the two arms of the cross will be the exact position of the bench mark. Locate your temporary bench mark outside the grid area at a place where it will not be dislodged during the dig-

ging. This is especially important if more than one season is to be spent on the site. A feature such as a large rock or a pavement can act as a base for a temporary bench mark. Or use an 18- or 24-inch steel rod sunk into the ground. If no permanent place can be found within a convenient distance from the site, construct one. (Figure 6.3). The concrete block can be made simply by digging a hole in the ground 50x50x50 centimetres, filling it with cement, and setting an iron pipe or an iron rod into it. A known elevation can be scratched into the top of the block to form a permanent bench mark.

When the dig is finished, a temporary bench mark can be related to a permanent bench mark near the site, or to some established feature such as the centre of a road or the corner of a bridge or church building. A list of established bench marks in each map quadrant of Canada can be obtained from the Geodetic Survey of Canada, Ottawa.

LABELLING THE GRID UNITS

When the grid stakes have been placed the grid intervals can be labelled for record-keeping.

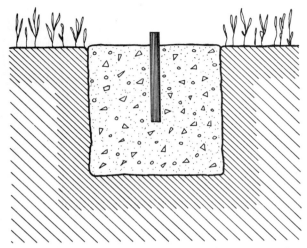

Figure 6.3. Constructing a permanent bench mark for a site that will be worked a number of seasons.

Beginning at the grid south (not to be confused with true south which is obtained from a compass) assign upper case letters in a south to north direction from A to Z (omitting the confusing letters I and O); the intervals from grid east to west are assigned arabic numerals from 1 onward.

The squares of an area are identified by lower case letters, beginning with the letter a in the southeast square and proceeding in a clock-wise direction to square d in the northeast corner of the area.

This system of labelling the grid units is illustrated in figure 6.1. Square C2a is located from the south to north at the interval letter C and from the east to west at the interval numbered 2. The particular square in question is in the southeast corner of the area and designated with the letter a.

Write the designation for each square on the grid stakes with an indelible black felt-tip pen so that the excavation crews can refer to this information when making out tags or completing record forms.

At this point an exhaustive surface collection should be done of all areas within the grid system. The material collected may give a hint of where to begin excavation. It should be labelled according to the square it comes from and marked "surface".

APPROACHES TO EXCAVATION

An experienced archaeologist attempts to evaluate the benefits of digging a given square before he begins to work on it. Since time is usually short, he begins with the most important squares and works to the less important. As a square is being dug the area supervisor should evaluate the information being uncovered, and if necessary, change his tactics to avoid wasting effort and time.

There are a number of methods of finding the most important squares and obtaining the best results in the time available. We will discuss several of these.

Plate 6.2. An area under excavation using test pits and a subsidiary baulk. Where the baulk is no longer necessary it has been removed to show the stones of an earlier building.

Test Pits

At an extensive site, where the limits of occupation are not known beforehand, you can begin by excavating a 1 by 1-metre area of one corner of a series of squares. This will give a rapid and orderly probe of the site and help to establish the limits of occupation. Later you can select those squares with the most significant evidence and dig these first, using the test pits as a guide to the removal of each layer from the entire square. A series of test pits across a site will also establish the occupational sequence, and the relationship of layers and their artifacts, to the architectural features. Test pits should be used with other approaches, however, as the pits uncover so limited a part of the site that it is not possible to get a complete picture of the occupation.

Trenching

A trench is a long and narrow cut through the site, often along one of the major axes, or at right angles to one of them. Trenching is useful where there are a number of occupational periods at the site and a limited amount of time to explore them. You then examine the vertical occupational periods in great detail, sacrificing the information that is found by the greater horizontal exposure of each layer.

To establish a trench on a gridded site, excavate the same part of several adjacent squares. The dividing baulks may be kept intact while the trench is excavated, or they can be progressively removed as it goes deeper into the ground.

Plate 6.3. The quadrant excavation of the circular base of an annealing oven at the Napanee Glass Works, Napanee, Ontario.

Open Excavation

If a site has one occupational period you may want to excavate it so as to obtain as much horizontal exposure of the features as possible. In this case you will want to open a wide area, with the fewest possible baulks or other obstructions, in order to uncover the plan of the occupation. Open excavations have proved useful on sites that have been disturbed by cultivation or building construction, and, consequently, have lost the original layering of soil or debris. The prime objective of open excavation is to be able to locate and plan architectural features.

Small circular features such as the remains of a pottery kiln are best excavated using a modified square approach, shown in plate 6.3. The feature is divided into four quarters, with the baulks arranged so that their vertical faces give a continuous section through the centre of the feature, with one section being at right angles to the other. An ordinary grid pattern might not have baulks through the centre of the kiln and would therefore provide an inaccurate cross-section of the structure.

The next chapter introduces the techniques used to remove successive layers of soil and debris from the squares.

Chapter 7

EXCAVATING LAYERS AND ARCHITECTURAL FEATURES

All archaeological excavation is destructive; once the trowel has removed the evidence as it is preserved in the ground you cannot re-dig the site to correct errors or to fill omissions in field records. Because of the finality of all archaeological excavation, all diggers must have a thorough understanding of its principles.

The excavation of an historical site involves the systematic removal of layers of soil and debris that have accumulated as a result of human activity. Unlike the soil scientist, who is interested in the development of soil types and soil layers in nature, the archaeologist almost always confines his interest to those layers that man has disturbed or changed in some way.

In archaeology, the layering of soils is called *stratification,* a word used by geologists to describe the layering of the crust of the earth. Likewise, the vertical pattern of successive layers is called the *stratigraphy* of the site. The excavation of an historic site has frequently been called "dirt" archaeology to indicate the emphasis placed on digging successive layers of soil and debris rather than limiting the investigation to a documentation or non-digging search.

It is in the context of the layers of soil and debris that datable artifacts can provide meaningful information. The dating of all the artifacts from each successive layer provides a range of dates for each successive individual layer at a site. As architectural features are associated with specific layers of soil and debris, establishing the dates of these layers enables the excavator to date the various phases of the feature. Therefore, it is of prime importance not

to sever an architectural feature from its surrounding layers by digging a hole around the feature or by digging a trench parallel to its face. When a feature is separated from its adjacent soil layers it may be impossible to date it.

Note also that the date attributable to a layer is not necessarily different from that of another layer directly above or below it. This is often the case at sites with a short history of human occupation, where, for instance, a building may have been built and destroyed within a short time. The artifacts associated with both the construction and destruction phases may give us essentially the same date, yet the soil characteristics of the two phases will differ markedly. In such cases, grouping certain layers may help to establish and simplify the successive time scale for the overall site.

As layers are often sloping or of uneven thickness the same layer may be encountered in various locations at different depths. Consequently, the vertical distance of an object from the surface tells us nothing by itself of its date or the layer of its origin. For this reason do not excavate by arbitrarily determined increments on historical sites. Figure 7.2 illustrates the importance of digging by layers rather than measured units. The number on the side of the figure indicates the depth in centimetres to which the site would have been dug after the removal of successive 10-centimetre increments. The layers in the square are not level, and removing the increment between 10 and 20 centimetres will mix material from layers 2 and 3. The material in the increment between 30 and 40 centimetres con-

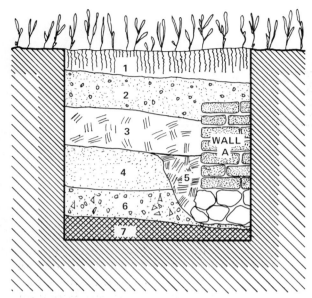

Figure 7.1a.

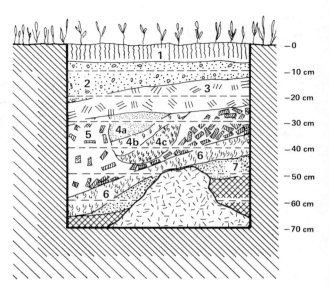

Figure 7.2. Excavation by arbitrary levels will mix material from different layers thus making stratigraphic intepretation impossible.

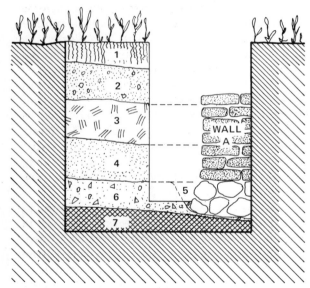

Figure 7.1b.

The layers adjacent to wall A have been severed by trenching parallel to the face of the wall. If the archaeologist assumes that the artifacts in layer 4 are contemporary with the wall, he will have made an error in interpretation as Wall A (shown in Fig. 7-1b) is actually cut into layer 4 and the material in layer 3 is contemporary with the wall.

tains artifacts from five different layers, including layers 4a, 4b and 4c of the pit and layers 5 and 6. If the artifacts are found to cover a large time-span, then mixing them will make it virtually impossible to assign them correctly to their respective layers. The principle of excavating by layers requires that you dig and record the layers as they are deposited, remembering that a layer is a natural or man-made deposit and not a level. (By definition, a *level* is a horizontal measurement above or below a fixed point.)

The dates of the artifacts in a layer can tell us the date before which the layer could not have been deposited. For example, a Canadian coin dated 1885 could not have been deposited in a layer before 1885, as it had not yet been minted, although it might have been deposited in 1886 or even 1910, as coins, like other typical artifacts, are used over a period of years. Many objects, such as porcelain, are manufactured with the same pattern over an extended period of time. In this case the range of possible dates during which the porcelain might have been manufactured would be wide. As a result, the discovery of such a porcelain sherd without other data could indicate a known time span but could not be used to determine a specific year for a layer or feature.

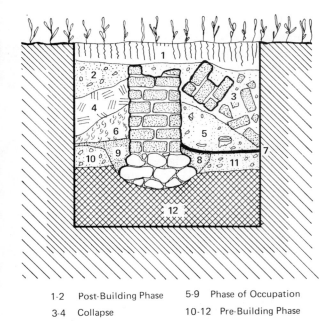

| 1-2 | Post-Building Phase | 5-9 | Phase of Occupation |
| 3-4 | Collapse | 10-12 | Pre-Building Phase |

Figure 7.3. A section showing the history of a wall.

The interpretation of the history of a wall is shown in figure 7.3. The wall (Wall A) was built by digging into soil layers 10, 11, 12 to make a builder's trench for its foundations. After the stone foundation was built, the space between the wall and the surrounding soil was filled (layers 8 and 9) and compacted to protect the foundation and to form an earthen floor surface (layer 7). If a coin dated 1815 were accidently dropped when the fill of layer 8 was placed in the builder's trench, then we have evidence that the wall was built in or after 1815. Since the floor acts as a barrier to any objects being inserted beneath it, unless this is done intentionally or the floor is broken by a pit, we say the floor "seals" off all the layers beneath it. An 1823 coin found in layer 5 above the floor and the 1815 coin in the builder's trench enable us to say that the structure was built after 1815 but before 1823. As more evidence is uncovered it may be possible to shorten this range of dates for the building of the structure. The building was abandoned or destroyed and the debris from this was allowed to partially fill the site (layers 2 through 6). Artifacts from these debris layers give us a range of dates after the abandonment of the building. The abandoned site was covered by weeds, and a thick layer of organic matter has continued to accumulate up to the present time (layer 1).

Not every site is as simple and straightforward. The stones or bricks from the ruins of a wall might have been partially or completely dismantled, or re-used elsewhere, leaving as the only evidence of the former structure the outline of the builder's trench. A site may also have walls with a series of phases, one upon the other, each representing the rebuilding, repair or expansion of the existing structure. It is then necessary to assign to each building phase the layer or layers that are associated with it. If careful records are kept as a structure is being uncovered, the evidence of the relationships between the layers and a structure can be preserved. These records will consist of photographs of the layers where they abut on the structure, field notes, measurements of the wall and layers, plans of the structure, and scaled drawings of the stratigraphy of the baulks where they are intersected by the feature.

In a few instances the feature may be in the middle of a square and not intersected by a baulk. Then the area supervisor must establish a subsidiary baulk (figure 7.4) between the feature and a regular baulk, with the subsidiary baulk at right angles to a regular baulk or a feature whenever possible. The subsidiary baulk is retained in the square as long as excavation of the structure continues.

The Probe Trench

Since it is not usually possible to identify a layer before digging it, the archaeologist uses a probe trench (a form of the test pit) to identify the vertical layering in a small part of the square before extensive horizontal excavation. Usually a probe trench is no more than 20 per cent of the area of a square. The probe trench tells the excavator whether changes in the stratification are significant or merely localized discolourations or deposits within a layer. A layer is rarely homogeneous in structure and texture; localized variations must be examined and interpreted before time is spent separating and treating each variation as a distinct layer.

The probe trench should be placed at right angles to any visible architectural feature in the

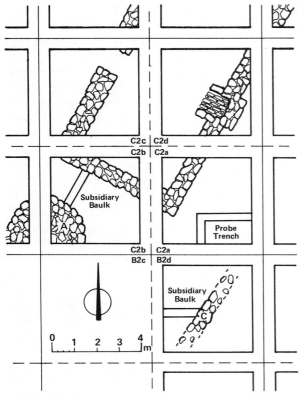

Figure 7.4. A site showing the use of subsidiary baulks. In C2b a subsidiary baulk joins feature A to the wall in the northeast corner of the area. In square B2d the second subsidiary baulk is used to connect wall C to the west baulk in order to retain the stratigraphic sequence. Square C2a has a probe trench in the southeast corner of the square.

square. Note that the probe trench of square C2a shown in figure 7.4 also has a subsidiary baulk between the sides of the probe trench and the remainder of the square. This baulk prevents the contamination of the layers in the probe trench by material from outside the trench. Remove the subsidiary baulk as the excavation goes deeper into the ground, retaining sufficient baulk that two layers are visible at any time. You will then be able to relate the layer you are removing to the layer just removed.

Begin the probe trench by removing the sod and all the loose topsoil underneath until changes in the nature of the soil indicate the top of a second layer. As the first layer of the probe trench is removed, put any artifacts in it in a container with a tag indicating the layer in which they were found. Remember to put the artifacts collected from layers of a probe trench in buckets separate from those collected during the excavation of the rest of the layer in the square. Doing so will help prevent confusion when you are attempting to evaluate the evidence from the layers of the square, as the numbering of layers of the probe trench may be different from that of the rest of the square. This is due to the fact that digging of the probe trench is exploratory and may involve the mixing of layers, while subsequent work in the rest of the square allows more precise separation of layers.

Remove the material from each layer of the probe trench from the square and sieve it before putting it in the dump. Small artifacts that are unnoticed in the square are often found by sieving the soil. The size of mesh of the sieve will vary according to the type of layer being removed, with a fine soil requiring a mesh opening no larger than 0.25 inches and a coarse soil requiring a mesh opening of 0.5 inches or larger.

When the top of the second layer has been exposed throughout the area of the probe trench, it should be cleaned to remove any remaining dirt from the previous layer. Prepare new bucket tags and buckets to receive artifacts removed from the second layer, and insert a baulk tag in the baulks of the probe trench to mark the layers (see page 83). The procedure for the removal of the second layer then follows that already discussed. After two distinct layers have been identified in the probe trench, you may want to begin to remove the uppermost layer from the rest of the square. However, the probe trench should always be at least one layer deeper than the remainder of the square throughout the excavation, as the results of the probe trench provide an indication of the layer sequence in the square, and an indication of what may be expected in layers not yet uncovered. The probe trench results should be studied by the area supervisor and director before work on the rest of the square begins.

In digging, an experienced archaeologist removes only small amounts of a layer at a time, carefully working through it with his hands to locate any small artifacts. The square must be kept clean at all times, except for the area immediately around the diggers. You cannot maintain control over the accuracy of digging if small

Plate 7.1. A probe trench at the Huron Pottery site with each layer labelled in the baulks.

piles of loose dirt are permitted to accumulate through the square. The preparation of baulk and bucket tags for each layer is discussed later in this chapter.

SOILS AND SOIL LAYERS

A site can be correctly excavated only if the excavator is able to recognize, identify, and describe each distinct layer of soil or debris as it is encountered. The description of each layer should include the colour, texture, and quantity and distribution of inclusions. Debris layers are described according to the same procedures as soil layers.

Soil Colour

The soil colour can be determined by comparing a sample of soil, either wet or dry, with chips of standard colour. In the field the soil is usually described when at its maximum wetness. The Munsell Soil Colour Charts, produced by Munsell Products, of Baltimore, Maryland, U.S.A., are favoured by soil scientists in North America and used by many others throughout the world.

In the Munsell system a colour is described by a three-part formula consisting of notations for hue, value and chroma, which are combined in this order to give a colour designation.

Hue

The hue is the dominant colour of the spectrum. The whole colour spectrum is divided into ten hues from red-purple (RP) through red (R), yellow-red (YR), yellow (Y), green-yellow (GY), green (G), blue-green (BG), blue (B), purple-blue (PB), to purple (P). Each hue is divided into ten parts. The 0 value of each hue classification is the same as the 10 value of the previous hue. For example, 0YR is the same as 10R, 5YR is the mid-point of the yellow in the YR hue, and 10YR coincides with the zero point of the next hue (Y). The standard binder of Munsell soil colour charts comes equipped with charts for hue 10R to 5Y, although additional colour charts can be produced to order.

Value

The value is the particular shade of the colour, that is, the lightness or darkness compared to absolute white. Value consists of numbers from 0 for absolute black to 10 for absolute white. A colour of value 5/ is mid-way between absolute black and absolute white. One of 7/ is less dark, 70 per cent of the way from black to white and mid-way between 6/ and 8/.

Chroma

The chroma refers to the purity of colour. Chroma is expressed by a number beginning from 0 (neutral grey) to a maximum of about 20 (pure).

To use the colour charts, place a soil sample behind the round hole separating two closely matching colour chips. The soil will rarely match a colour chip exactly, but it should be possible to indicate which colour is the closest.

The colour of the soil is written in the standard Munsell notation. The order is hue, value and chroma, with a space between the hue letter and the value number, and a slanted line between the numbers for value and chroma. The notation for hue 5YR, value 3 and chroma 4 is written as 5YR 3/4, a dark reddish brown.

Colours between two standard chips can be indicated by using the mid-point of the notations. The notation for a soil that is mid-way between the colour chips for 5 YR 3/4 and 5YR 4/4 would be 5YR 3.5/4; one mid-way between 5YR 4/4 and 5YR 4/5 would be 5YR 4/4.5. A soil with a colour that is mid-way between 5YR 5/2 and 7.5YR 6/4 would be 6.25YR 5.5/3.

If Munsell charts are not available you can produce a set of reference colours with the readily available and standardized artist's oil paints. The colours can be made light by mixing colour from the tube with an equal quantity of titanium white. In some cases the oil colours can be cross-indexed with the Munsell charts. For example, Indian red is Munsell colour designation 7.5R 2/8 while light Indian red is 7.5R 3/4; Naples yellow is 10YR 9/6 and light Naples yellow is 5Y 7/6.

One word of caution — whoever works with the colour charts must have normal colour vision!

Texture

Another soil characteristic which should be evaluated and recorded is the texture, the proportion of particle sizes in a soil. The Wentworth scale is commonly used in this classification. A set of sieves with small openings to screen the finer sized particles in the Wentworth scale can be obtained from the Canadian Laboratory Supplies Ltd., Toronto.

Wentworth Scale

clay	up to 0.031 millimetres
silt	0.031 - 0.0625 millimetres
sand	0.0625 - 2 millimetres
granule	2 - 4 millimetres
pebble	4 - 64 millimetres
cobble	64 - 256 millimetres
boulder	256 millimetres and up

The texture designations for soils are determined by the predominate amounts of the three smallest particles in the Wentworth scale—sand, silt and clay. When all three of these size fractions are present in sizeable amounts the term *loam* is used to describe the soil. A *sandy clay* designation denotes a soil which is predominantly clay but has some sand. A *sandy clay loam* is similar to a "sandy clay" except it contains more silt.

Soil texture can be estimated by taking a sample of the soil between the forefinger and thumb and rubbing. If the soil is loose and single-grained and falls apart easily when dry, it is a sand. If the soil is fine, forms hard lumps when dry, and is sticky, plastic, and shiny when wet, it is a clay. Silt will form a print when pressed with a finger. A loam has a gritty feeling, yet is smooth and slightly plastic. It will form a cast when wet but this requires careful handling.

The twelve main soil textures are shown on the U.S. Department of Agriculture soil texture triangle (figure 7.5). The definition of the basic soil texture classes are given in the USDA *Soil Survey Manual,* and "Soil Classification, A Comprehensive System", 7th Approximation, Soil Conservation Service, USDA, 1960.

In the triangle the respective percentages of sand, silt and clay in the sample will indicate the soil designation. Through field experience you will soon learn to identify soil texture without difficulty.

The distribution of soil particles of granule or larger size should be included in a description of the soil layer. These particles should be measured, if possible, with a pocket rule so their size can be included in the field notes.

Inclusions

So far in the discussion, debris layers have been described along with soil layers. The major distinction between the two comes in describing the inclusions in the debris layer. Brick fragments, mortar, or other identifiable constituents should be measured and the size-range of these materials recorded. The identification of all inclusions in a debris layer will help you interpret the meaning of a layer. A thick layer of brick or stone may indicate the destruction of a building; a baked layer of clay may indicate a floor; a soft layer of organic matter with fragments of wood may indicate the location of a post hole, a wooden floor, or a wooden building.

LABELLING LAYERS AND ARCHITECTURAL FEATURES

The previous chapter introduced a system for designating the horizontal units of a site. This system can now be expanded vertically to in-

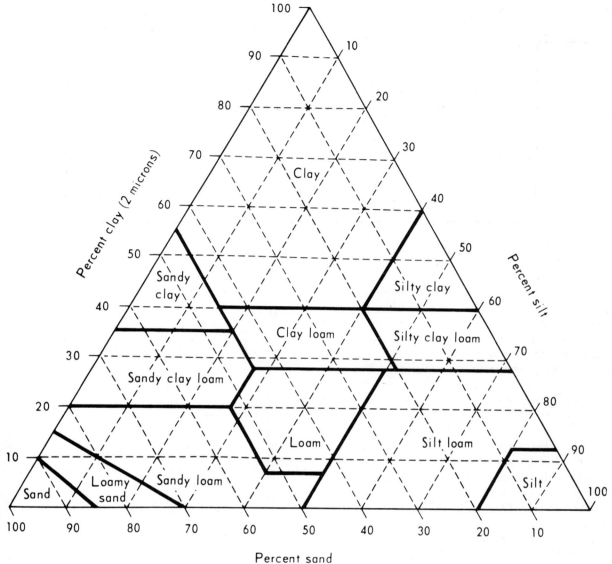

Figure 7.5. A soil texture triangle. Courtesy U.S. Department of Agriculture

clude all layers and features encountered in a square.

Figure 7.6 illustrates a method of labelling layers and features of square C2a. The sod and loose topsoil of the square is the first layer and is recorded as layer number 1. The next layer is divided by a wall (Wall A) into two parts. The materials found in each part of a layer divided by a feature must be kept separate, because the sections on each side of the feature may have had a different history. One of the parts of the second layer continues the consecutive number-

ing system for the square and is labelled layer number 2, while the other part is distinguished from this by using the number 3. These designations are reflected in the baulk tags and artifact buckets.

The next layer under the layer numbered 2 is the top of a pit, which, although it cuts vertically into two different layers, is itself treated as a layer and receives a layer number. A pit is excavated in the order in which it was excavated at the site. In figure 7.6 the pit was made after layer 5 (into which it cuts) had been deposited, but

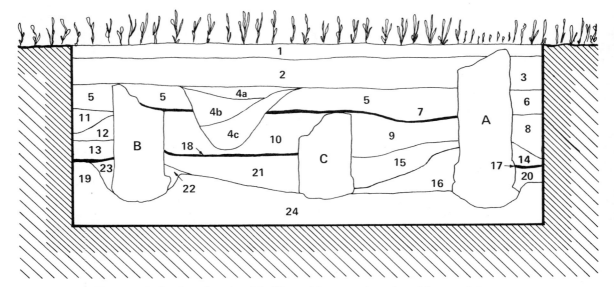

Figure 7.6. Section showing labelling of layers, pit and architectural features.

before layer 2, which covers the pit. If a pit has internal layers, these should be designated by the layer number followed by a lower case arabic letter, beginning with a. In figure 7.6 the layers in the pit are 4a, 4b and 4c. After the pit is removed the layer or layers into which it cuts can be removed. The process of numbering layers or units of layers continues in the square until undisturbed sub-soil (layer number 24) is reached. It is important to excavate all layers, including floors, as distinct units and to separate the artifacts from each.

Architectural features such as the remains of a wall or other structure are given upper case letters, beginning with the letter A and omitting the confusing letters I and O. In figure 7.6 the walls are labelled A, B and C, in the order in which they were first uncovered. When a number of walls are found in one square it is then possible to describe their relationship by referring to the letter designations.

Labelling the Baulks

The simple but accurate method of labelling layers in squares would be routine if it were not for the problem of labelling layers of the baulks. At most excavations the baulks are removed before the field work is completed but after the layers of the adjacent squares have been

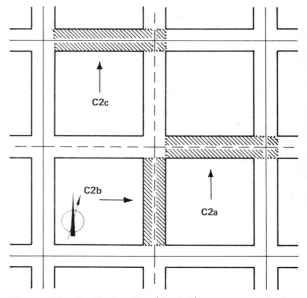

Figure 7.7. As the baulks (shaded) are removed, the artifacts should be labelled according to the square containing the arrow.

removed. In many cases the numbering of the layers of two adjacent squares will be different, as one area supervisor may have identified and excavated more layers than another (although this does not mean that he has been more accurate in his identification and evaluation of the stratigraphy). The problem is then to label the layers from the baulks. In figure 7.7 one possible system is illustrated.

Here the layers of the north and east baulks of the square are labelled in the same sequence as the layer numbers in the square. For example, the north baulk in square C2a would be excavated using the adjacent layer numbers of square C2a; likewise, the east baulk of C2b would be designated using the adjacent layers in the square C2b. The exception to this convention for labelling the baulks would be for those found against the south and west edges of the grid. Here the south baulk would have to be identified with the square immediately to its north and the west baulk would have to be identified with the square immediately to its east.

In order to distinguish baulk material from that of the square itself, the artifact buckets from the baulk are labelled with an additional entry of either NB for north baulk, EB for east baulk, or SB and WB for south and west baulks, respectively. For example, the artifacts from the third layer of the east baulk of square C2a in figure 7.7 would be placed in a bucket and tagged C2a3 EB.

PREPARING BAULK AND BUCKET TAGS

During the dig an area supervisor is responsible for preparing tags for the baulks and the artifact buckets. When the supervisor first identifies a layer in the square or probe trench he should prepare a tag to mark the top of the layer and place it in the baulk. Bucket tags for the artifacts

of each layer should then be designated according to the soil layer shown on the baulk tag.

The Baulk Tag

As successive layers are located in the baulk they should be labelled with a tag. This tag marks the upper vertical limits of the layer at the time it is dug. The area supervisor should not move a tag once the layer has been located in the baulk, even though he may see at a later time that its location is incorrect. A baulk tag indicates to the person making a scaled drawing of the face of the baulk the numbers which the excavator has assigned to each layer and its corresponding artifact buckets at the time the layer was removed. Baulk tags are a handy reference guide for the digging and for further labelling of the layers.

The baulk tag should contain the following information: site and year, area, square and layer. These should be printed large enough that the tags can be read in photographs (if only with a magnifying lens). A sample tag is shown in figure 7.8. Whenever possible place baulk tags in a vertical row near the corner of each baulk of the square, or where a layer first appears in a baulk, and secure them with nails so they will not fall out or be blown away.

The Artifact Bucket Tag

The area supervisor should prepare two tags for each artifact bucket before the bucket is used in the excavations. One of the tags should be attached by string to the bucket, while the second tag is placed loose inside. Each tag should contain the following information: site (abbreviated to two or three upper case letters) and year, area, square, layer, bucket number, date, and the initials of the recorder. Buckets removed from the square should be given consecutive numbers and a record of the buckets from each square kept in a separate register.

If a bucket is used for artifacts from a probe trench or baulk indicate this with an additional entry of PT for probe trench, EB for east baulk, or NB for north baulk, etc. For example, if bucket number 9 from square C2a is for artifacts from the probe trench of layer 2, prepare a new bucket, numbered 10, for the artifacts from the remainder of layer 2.

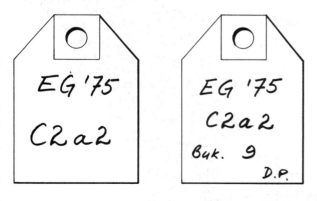

a. Baulk Tag   **b. Artifact Bucket Tag**

Figure 7.8. Tags for labelling baulks (a) and artifact buckets (b).

It is a good practice not to use an artifact bucket for more than one day's work. As a matter of policy assign a new number every day, even though excavation may be continuing in the same layer as the day before. When a bucket is re-used, the chance of mixing or re-interpreting materials is greater. Also, when new buckets are issued every day the technical staff processing the finds can complete their work the same day the artifacts are removed from the soil.

If an artifact is especially fragile, particularly useful in dating, unusual, or for other reasons worthy of special handling, separate it from other recovered materials and place it in a special container with a separate tag identical to that of the bucket tag. Another tag is attached to or placed with the artifact before it is put in the container. Mark the outside of the bag or box (both lid and bottom) with the same information as is shown on the tag inside the container. The bag or box should be filled with loose packing and securely closed to prevent damage to the artifact. When the artifact buckets are processed in the field laboratory these special artifacts will be listed as objects, entered in an object register and given an object number. More will be said about the handling of objects in Chapter 9.

THE LEVEL AND ITS USE

No other piece of scientific equipment is as important or as useful on an historical site as a level. Although a dig may be able to function without a transit, without a reliable level it cannot get through a day. If you do not own a level and cannot afford to invest in a new one, it may be possible to borrow one from a nearby university, college, or construction firm. If all these sources fail, a rental agency will provide one by the week.

A level determines the differences in elevation

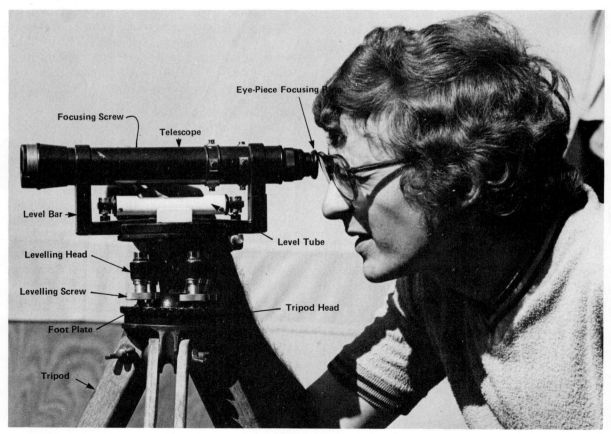

Plate 7.2. A level in use with basic parts labelled.

between positions, either between positions solely within individual squares, or between the temporary bench mark (datum point) and one or more points on the site. This allows more precise evaluation of vertical relationships than the unaided eye affords. The level can be used to establish contour lines on uneven sites in order to define the shape of mounds or depressions, and to record the height or depth of layers or architectural features. Levels taken on layers in a square can be correlated with those of layers in adjacent squares and a continuous cross-section through the site worked out. By regular recording of levels for all layers and features you can check the accuracy of scaled drawings of the faces of baulks (and should drawings or plans of the dig be lost or accidentally destroyed these records can often be used to reconstruct them.) Architectural features appear on plans as ''flat''. With the use of the level, their relative heights at various places can be recorded.

The Dumpy Level

The simplest type of level is the dumpy level, the parts of which are shown in plate 7.2. A telescope with a spirit-level tube is attached to a parallel base plate by means of three or four levelling screws. The telescope contains a series of lenses that enable a person looking through the eyepiece to read the divisions on a surveyor's rod held at a distance. The telescope is focused by a screw on its right-hand side. Inside is a diaphragm with two fine cross-hairs. These cross-hairs enable the viewer to sight on the surveyor's rod and take a reading at the point where the two hairs intersect. These cross-hairs can be brought into focus by turning the eyepiece, but once they have been focused it may be necessary to re-focus on the rod, using the telescope screw. The spirit-level tube is graduated; when the bubble remains in the centre of the tube as the telescope is rotated completely once, the level is ready to use.

Step-by-step instructions for the use of the dumpy level are given below.

SETTING UP THE LEVEL

1. Open the tripod legs so that they are at an angle of about 60 degrees with the ground. If the legs are too close the instrument may topple in a strong wind; too far apart they are often dislodged during use.

2. Remove the dumpy level from its case with one hand holding the telescope and the other hand under the base of the instrument. Always use two hands to carry the instrument to avoid the possibility of it slipping.

3. Mount the dumpy level on the tripod legs by holding the instrument with one hand on the telescope and the other on the base plate. Gently screw the level onto the tripod head in a clockwise direction until it is firmly attached. It is important to prevent the threads from getting crossed.

4. To level-up the instrument, adjust the tripod legs so that by visual observation the instrument is relatively level. This will eliminate the need to make major adjustments of the levelling screws.

5. Move the telescope so that it is aligned with two of the three or two of the four levelling screws. Grip these screws with the forefinger and thumb of each hand. When one hand is on each levelling screw, bringing both thumbs together causes the bubble to move to one direction; moving the thumbs away from each other moves the bubble in the opposite direction. When the bubble in the spirit-level is centred the telescope is level over the two screws.

6. Now rotate the telescope 90 degrees so that the telescope is aligned with the third screw. Repeat the directions above. When the telescope has been levelled in this manner, return it to the first position and check to see that it is still level. Continue to make any necessary corrections until the bubble is in the centre of the spirit-level tube when the instrument is revolved to any position. The line through the axis of the telescope and the two cross-hairs is called the *line of collimation*. When the instrument has been levelled its line of collimation is horizontal.

7. It is important to make sure that the levelling screws are secured against the lower base plate. If the screws are loose then the instrument will wobble and not remain horizontal.

Plate 7.3. Using a level to measure differences in elevation at a site. The rod should be held firmly with both hands, taking care not to shield the numbers on the face of the rod.

FOCUSING THE TELESCOPE

1. First, it is necessary to adjust the level so that the reading on the staff is parallel to the plane of the cross-hairs. This prevents what is called *parallax*, an error due to the change of viewing position. Turn the telescope focus screw so that the telescope is just out of focus. Then carefully focus the eye-piece on the cross-hairs by gently turning the eye-piece with the forefinger and thumb of one hand until the cross-hairs are in focus. The dumpy level has now been corrected for parallax.

2. Turn the telescope in the direction of the surveyor's rod. Now focus the telescope using the focusing knob on the right side of the instrument. Every time the rod is moved to a new position the dumpy level will have to be re-focused.

3. Check again for a possible parallax error. If the cross-hairs remain constant as the telescope is focused with reference to the divisions on the surveyor's rod when viewing through the eye-piece, then there is no parallax. If, however, the cross-hairs appear to move away from the divisions of the rod, then the procedure for correcting parallax in step 1 should be repeated.

USING THE DUMPY LEVEL

1. When the instrument is level and has been checked for parallax, it is ready for use. Start by having an assistant hold the rod on the bench mark, or datum point. Record the figure that is seen when the cross-hairs meet the rod. It will be necessary to become familiar with the divisions of a metric surveyor's rod. The rod man should confirm the position where the meter reading was taken by the reader. He can do this by moving his fingers up the rod until he intersects the point of collimation. When his fingers appear on the section of the rod being sighted on, he can check and confirm the reading. This first reading from the instrument to the bench mark is called

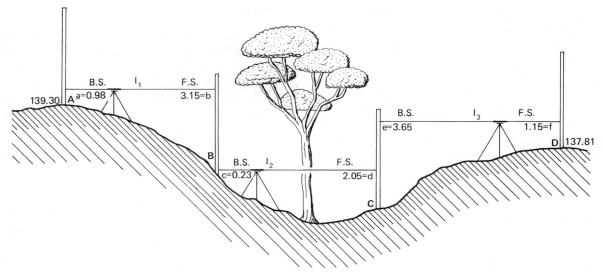

Figure 7.9. The difference in elevation between the resting point of the rod at positions A and D can be measured using the level and surveyor's rod. Place the rod at point A and set up the instrument at I_1 so it is possible to view the rod at point A through the telescope of the level. The reading on the rod at point A is taken from the telescope. This reading is a back sight (B.S.). The reading on the rod should be recorded as this gives the height of the instrument (H.I.) at I_1. The rod should then be moved to a new position and forward sight (F.S.) taken on the rod at this new position. The reading on the rod at position B is subtracted from the H.I. to give the elevation of the point where the rod is resting. The instrument is then moved to I_2 and a B.S. is made to point B and the reading added to the elevation of B to give the new H.I. The procedure is repeated in this manner until the instrument is in position to take a final F.S., which will give the elevation of D. The elevation of point A can then be compared to that of point D and the difference calculated by subtracting A from D. The calculations of a theoretical traverse across the depression shown in the above figure are as follows:

Ht. at A	*139.30 metres*	*139.30 metres*
Ht. of I_1	*(139.30+a)*	*(139.30+0.98)*
Ht. at B	*(139.30+a)-b*	*(139.30+0.98)-3.15*
Ht. of I_2	*(139.30+a)-b+c*	*(139.30+0.98)-3.15+0.23*
Ht. at C	*(139.30+a)-b+c-d*	*(139.30+0.98)-3.15+0.23-2.05*
Ht. of I_3	*(139.30+a)-b+c-d+e*	*(139.30+0.98)-3.15+0.23-2.05+3.65*
Ht. at D	*(139.30+a)-b+c-d+e-f*	*(139.30+0.98)-3.15+0.23-2.05+3.65-1.15*

Difference between A and D is 139.30-137.81=-1.49, therefore D is 1.49 metres below point of resting of rod at A.

a backsight, and the value obtained from a backsight gives you the height of the instrument relative to the bench mark. This value must be recorded beside any readings taken with the level in this position, and another backsight obtained for readings taken from each different position. The readings should be entered in a level register or a level book can be purchased at any store selling surveying equipment.

2. There are several sources of error to avoid in reading the surveyor's rod. Typical mistakes occur when the rod is not fully extended, placed in a position where it sinks into the ground, or when the rod man does not hold the rod vertical.

3. Move the rod to the first position on the site

where a reading is to be taken. Record the reading in the level register or in the level book under the column called *intermediate sights*. In the level register there should also be a brief description of the siting point. In a level book there is space on the facing page for a drawing to indicate the position of all readings.

The reduced level of each position is its distance above or below the temporary bench mark. This value is entered under "D" in the level register or under "reduced level" in the level book.

4. If readings are to be taken on positions not in view of the level, it will be necessary to re-set the instrument at a new location. At most historical digs it is usually possible to re-set the instrument, take another backsight to the bench mark and then continue to take readings, adjusting each reading to obtain the reduced level. The last reading of the level before the instrument is re-set in a new location is called the *foresight*.

If it is not possible to take readings with reference to the original bench mark, a procedure called *series levelling*, in which the foresight is used as the backsight or bench mark for the instrument in a new position, is useful. The technique of series levelling is not discussed here but can be found in most elementary books on surveying.

5. Check the instrument bubble at frequent intervals to be sure it is still level. It is easy for the instrument to be dislodged or unbalanced, and care should be taken to keep the instrument level during use.

The Use of the Level in Excavation

During a typical day on a site the dumpy level will be used to take readings on both layers and features. A member of the technical staff will use the instrument and will depend on the area supervisor to tell him where the levels are to be taken. The readings are entered in the level register and later transferred to the excavation record sheet for the particular layer being removed. In excavating layers and features the level is used as follows:

LAYERS

1. After the grid has been set out on the site, take levels on the surface at each corner of the squares. If the surface of the site is very uneven, you may have to take a level at measured distances across the site in order to make a contour map. (Further information on making contour maps is given in chapter 4.)

2. Take levels in the four corners and in the centre of a square on the top of each layer before it is excavated. If a layer is excavated over a number of days, levels should be taken before the day's work on the layer begins, at the end of each day's work, and finally, after the layer has been completely removed. Any rapid change in the slope or direction of a layer should also be indicated with levels. Finally, when the excavation of a square is completed, indicate the bottom of the square by taking levels to show the limit of the excavation.

3. Levels are taken along floors, and at the top and bottom of pits, post holes, or other recognizable disturbances.

ARCHITECTURAL FEATURES

Take levels on the top and founding layers of all architectural features, along the entire length of a feature and at the top and bottom where it enters the baulks. (The *founding level* is the level underneath the lowest course of stone or brick of the feature.) Levels should be taken wherever there are noticeable changes in the height of the feature, and on the top of all layers associated with the feature at points where the layers and feature meet. This will let you construct an accurate elevation drawing later.

The dumpy level is one of the simpler forms of level; there are newer instruments, that level automatically. The procedures described in this chapter will require modification for other instruments, but these adjustments should not be major and can be learned from any elementary book on surveying or from the instrument manual.

As the dig progresses you will gather a large amount of information about the site, written notes, photographs, and drawings of the baulks and architecture. Recording and organizing this information is the subject of chapter 8.

Chapter 8

RECORDING INFORMATION DURING THE EXCAVATION

The records made during the dig are the primary source of information on the material discovered, and the basis for your published excavation report. No amount of afterthought, hearsay, or conjecture can substitute for carefully recorded factual observations. Without them you will produce nothing but a guide for the collector, or a local history decorated with interesting artifacts of uncertain origin. It is no secret in archaeological circles that inadequate records are the most common excuse for not publishing one's results. All potential leaders of archaeological digs should develop coherent, efficient and comprehensive procedures for recording information. The director of an excavation should establish a routine that will ensure that site supervisors and technical department staff will carry out the record-keeping duties as required.

The basic types of dig records are: the records of the evidence pertaining to stratigraphy and architectural features; drawings of all architectural features; drawings of the faces of the baulks; and photographs.

RECORDING STRATIGRAPHY AND ARCHITECTURAL FEATURES

The basic form for all observations on stratigraphy and architectural features is the field notebook. A hard-covered notebook with graph and lined pages opposite each other is the more traditional form, and can be purchased from school or university stationery suppliers. The pages are numbered and sewn together so they will not be misplaced or loosened. All stratigraphy and architectural features are drawn on the graph pages, while a log of the description and contents of all layers is entered on the opposite, lined pages. Another popular format for field notes is individual record sheets used with a clip-board and placed in a three-ring binder. This format is more flexible than the hardcover notebook, as only individual sheets need to be taken to the field, reducing the risk of losing the complete excavation record for a square. Unless the sheets are made of heavy paper, however, they will tear and pull out of the binder. It is a good idea to have the completed notes, whether in bound or loose-leaf, photographed or photocopied. You should also consider having all field notebooks and drawings microfilmed, for added protection against loss and for permanent storage. Deposited in an archives or local library, microfilm records would be easily available to researchers.

A separate excavation record sheet is used for each different layer or architectural feature encountered in a square. Start it as soon as a layer or feature is recognized, and enter *all* excavation information. In the upper right-hand corner is a space to indicate the site and year, area, square, layer number or architectural feature letter, the name of the recorder, and the dates during which the layer or feature was dug. The record sheet has the following parts:

PROGRESS AND DESCRIPTION OF EXCAVATION

This is a concise, detailed log of the step-by-step excavation of the layer or architectural feature. Each entry should be dated, since excavation may take several days. Include: (a) a description of the layer or architectural feature, including its relationship to other layers or features; (b) all the physical dimensions of the layer or architectural feature; (c) a description of the location of the layer or architectural feature relative to the two closest stakes in the square.

For soil and debris layers the physical description should include colour, texture, and nature of the contents (see chapter 7). If the layer is a surface or a floor, then the description should include information on its appearance—uneven, broken, sloping in a specific direction, patterned, etc. Describe the soil content 3 to 5 centimetres above a floor or surface also, as it may illustrate the contemporary uses of the structure. The relationship of a surface or floor to other layers and architectural features is important for interpreting the date and extent of such features during a particular phase of the site's history. Note any evidence that the floor or surface may have been cut by pits, walls or posts, or that the floor or surface has been repaired.

In excavating a house you will want to record the debris or soil layer on top of the floor, the layer beneath it, and whether there are any other surfaces or floors that can be shown to belong to the same phase. If an architectural feature is very large or complex, a number of measurements at various points along the base and top of the feature will have to be recorded.

PLAN OF LAYER OR ARCHITECTURAL FEATURE

On the front of the excavation record sheet is a graph on which to draw a scaled plan of a square during the excavation of each particular layer or feature. The grid north is indicated at the top of the page by an arrow pointing to the top right corner.

There are a number of details that can be included on the plan to show the course of the excavation. These include:

1. The extent of the layer or feature
2. The location of trial trenches
3. The location of any subsidiary baulks that were established in the square
4. The location and construction details of walls of buildings and other structures; walls should be drawn stone-for-stone or brick-for-brick.
5. Exact location of all elevations taken of the layer or architectural feature. The symbol⬧⟋ is used with all founding levels, and the symbol<> for all elevations taken on a layer or architectural feature.
6. Horizontal relationships of associated layers and architectural features. Indicate the larger number by circling it.
7. Exact location of the find spot of each object, measured from the two closest surveyed stakes in the area. The symbol X is used for the location of the object, and the object registry number placed beside it.
8. The area from which the artifacts in each bucket were collected, indicated by a sketch.

ELEVATIONS

Enter the elevations recorded during the excavation of the layer or architectural feature on the chart to the right of the graph. The information is obtained from the elevation register (see chapter 7) and includes the level number (No.), the reading from the level or transit (R), the height of the instrument (H.I.), and the difference between these last two values (D). The level number, and the difference, called the elevation, are placed on the plan at the point where the reading was taken. (A discussion of the level is found in chapter 7.)

ARTIFACT BUCKETS

List the artifact bucket numbers and describe the contents briefly on the excavation record form in the order in which they are removed. Each entry should include the area, square, and layer number and should agree with the information in the artifact bucket register, described in chapter 7.

OBJECTS

Each object from a layer is entered in numerical order in an object register, accompanied by a brief description of the object, the area, square,

OBJECTS

No.	A/S/L.	Bkt.	Description of Object	Init.
58	A5c5	21	fragment of medicine bottle	I.E.
59	A5c5	21	fragment of plaster of Paris mould	I.E.
60	A5c5	19	fragment of green bottle.	I.E.
61	A5c4	18	top of stoneware bottle marked "F.A.MEYER"	I.E.
62	A5c5	21	sprig-mould with grape cluster motif	D.N.
63	A5c5	19	beer bottle marked "Egmondville Brewery"	I.E.
64	A4d2	8	brick marked in frog "SPROAT"	I.E.
65	A5c4	18	base of water cooler 14" dia., glazed	I.E.
66	A5c5	21	sprig-mould with lion head motif	I.E.
67	A5c3	8	preserve jar lid; 10 cm. dia. yellow glaze	I.E.
68	A5c3	8	preserve jar lid; 10 cm. dia.; rust-brown glaze	I.E.
69	A4d3	4	table churn lid; 25 cm. dia.; yellow glaze	D.N.
70	A5c3	11	drain tile; 10 cm. dia; unglazed; 32 cm long	D.N.
71	A5c4	10	yellow glaze lid; 27.5 cm. dia.	D.N.
72	A5c4	10	churn top; 25 cm. dia; yellow glaze	I.E.
73	A5c4	10	churn top; 26 cm. dia.; rust-brown glaze	I.E.
74	A4c1	2	marked brick "KRUSE"	I.E.
75	A4c1	3	marked brick "SPROAT"	I.E.
76	A5b6NB	39	plaster of Paris mould of finial	B.F.
77	A5b6NB	39	unglazed clay finial w/plaster mould	B.F.
78	A5b6	38	1 gal. jug; yellow glaze	D.N.

NOTES

plaster of paris mould are badly deteriorated and have been permitted to dry slowly in shade. They have been specially wrapped to prevent damage. consult conservation technician about handling procedure; fragments of glass have no identifiable names or markings.

Plate 8.1. A sample object record sheet.

and layer, bucket number for the square, and the recorder's initials. Objects should be placed in a bag or box (which should also be labelled) and either kept with the artifact bucket or transferred to the field laboratory. The information recorded in the object register should be transferred to the excavation record sheet.

The excavation record sheet should also include the distance of the object from the two nearest stakes and the elevation of the object when first uncovered. A sample object register sheet is shown in plate 8.1. Do not move an object from its find spot without first consulting the area supervisor, as fragile objects are easily damaged by improper handling. Further information on the handling of objects is found in chapter 9.

PHOTOGRAPHS

List all photographs that show the particular layer or architectural feature. Each entry should include the roll and exposure numbers and indicate whether black and white or colour film was used. A separate photograph register is also maintained and is described later in this chapter.

SECTIONS AND PLANS

In addition to the drawings made on each excavation record sheet, there are "official" drawings that the area supervisor and the director prepare to represent the interpretation of the excavation to be used in the report. All such drawings should be listed on the excavation record sheet.

INTERPRETATIVE COMMENTS

A separate space is provided on the excavation record sheet for the note-keeper's personal interpretations. Here, he may want to suggest the nature and function of the layer or architectural feature, and its contribution to an understanding of the history of the site. Such speculative comments, however, should be kept separate from the factual observations.

Complete the record sheet entries the day the observations are made, not several days later when you may have forgotten the information. The area supervisor should retain the sheets at the end of each work day until the particular layer or architectural feature is completely removed. After each record sheet is completed and no longer of use for field excavations, send it to the field laboratory to be checked by the supervisor of the field laboratory and the director of the excavation. All entries on the record sheet should be written in India ink, or indelible-ink pen or ball-pen, and kept clean and dry.

FIELD DRAWING OF ARCHITECTURAL FEATURES

The drawings of the architectural features provide a site plan reproducing the shape of each feature and its location with respect to the entire site. The plan of individual buildings is supplemented by levels to correlate the height of the walls, floors and surfaces with founding levels for the structures. You can then construct frontal and side elevations. The permanent record of the stratigraphy is the scaled drawings of the faces of all baulks (sections), whether the four baulks forming the perimeter of the square or the subsidiary baulks or both. By correlating the plans of the architecture with those of the baulks, you can form a three-dimensional view of the site.

For all plans and section drawings use a scale to permit the drawings to be used as the basis for India ink drawings for the dig report. A scale of five centimetres on the drawing to one metre on the ground (1:20) is adequate for small sites, but a scale of 2 centimetres to the metre (1:50) would be required for larger structures. In all cases the scale used must appear on the drawing as both a ratio and a scale bar.

A plan showing the site grid and the corner stakes should be prepared before the digging begins, as you can use it as a base for further maps. The base plan should be attached firmly to a plane table or a drawing board. The architectural details of each square can be added either directly on the base plan, if the feature is likely to appear in all subsequent overlays, or on mylar overlays for layers that appear in only a part of the site. Separate overlays are also useful for sites with a large number of objects or elevations.

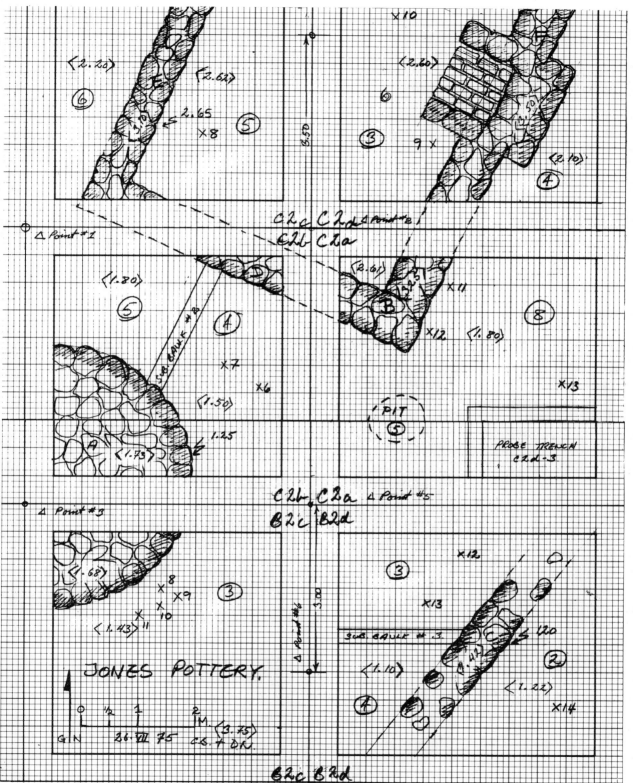

Figure 8.1. Finished field plan of a pottery site. This plan is now ready to be traced for publication.

Drawing the Plan

The details on the official plans of the dig include:

1. The location of all buildings and other structures; walls should be drawn stone-for-stone or brick-for-brick rather than as solid black space. An illustration of a stone-for-stone drawing of the foundations of a building, and the brick-for-brick drawing of another building is shown in figure 8.1.

2. Show elevations for the founding levels of all architectural features, as on the excavation record sheet. The symbol ⚡ should be used with all founding levels and the symbol <> for all elevations taken on a layer or architectural feature.

3. The horizontal relationships of associated layers and architectural features. Indicate a layer number by circling it.

4. The exact location of the find spot of each object, measured from the two closest surveyed stakes in the area. Use the symbol X for the location of the object, and beside it put an object register number.

Start plans and section drawing when buildings or layers are first uncovered in a square. The frequent updating of all plans during the course of the digging is an opportunity to develop explanations of the archaeological results and a strategy for further digging. Do not leave any drawings to the last days of the excavation, as the lack of time may result in shortcuts that will affect the quality of the plans.

Plate 8.2. Using stakes and strings, a 50 cm mapping grid is laid over a circular kiln base in preparation for planning.

You can plan architectural features such as walls by placing a datum line along the top length of the wall. The ends of the line should intersect the baulks, where they should be firmly attached. Place a cloth metric tape beside this datum line, with the zero point of the tape at one of the baulk edges. All stones or bricks can be measured by holding a small metal tape at right angles to the line and at measured distances along the datum line taking readings from the line to each of the outside edges of the wall. Then plot the measurements. Sketch individual stones or bricks by measuring and plotting their corner points. You can approximate the shapes by connecting these measured points, after carefully observing the apparent form of the stone or brick. If part of a wall is obstructed or too far below the datum line for direct measurement, use a plumb-bob. Holding a metal tape in one hand and the plumb-bob in the other, with the plumb-bob over the edge of a stone or brick, measure the horizontal distance from the string of the plumb-bob to the datum line.

As one worker takes measurements of a wall, a second can plot the readings on the graph paper. The exact location of both ends of the datum line over the wall should be indicated on the plan. The accuracy of this can be checked by measuring the actual length of the line over the wall with the length as indicated by the plan scale. They should be the same.

Architecture other than walls or linear features can be planned by using a square frame, which consists of a moveable grid of strings or wires, spaced ten centimetres from each other. Plate 8.3 shows a frame with an inside measurement of one square metre. The brickwork of the base of the kiln is being planned by placing the frame in a horizontal position in each of the one-metre grid squares set over the kiln. The bricks are drawn either by standing over the frame and sketching them on the plan or by having another worker estimate the distance measurements by visual observation of the strings. As before, these points are plotted on the drawing and the shape of the bricks and stones sketched. Finally, plans are labelled with the site, date, scale, conventional north, architectural feature letters, and the names of the planners. Upon completion compare the plans of a square

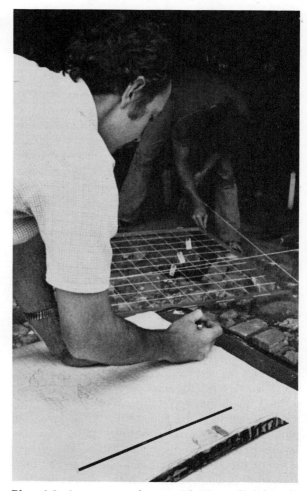

Plate 8.3. A one-metre frame with 10 cm divisions is laid over an architectural feature.

with the details on the excavation record sheets for all layers and architectural features involved. Any errors or omissions can then be corrected.

ARCHAEOLOGICAL SECTIONS

Draw each side of a baulk on a scaled plan, called a section. The purpose of this drawing is to show the stratigraphy revealed in the baulks of each square, and to provide a means of correlating the stratigraphy of one square with that of the squares adjacent to it.

The scale used in the section will depend on the amount of detail to be shown. You should plot thin layers on a scale large enough to show each layer distinctly. Conversely, where thick layers are encountered use a small scale. It is desirable, however, to draw all sections to the same scale, e.g. 1:20, if this can be done without affecting the presentation of the stratigraphy.

To establish a horizontal datum line, place a taut string parallel to the face of the baulk. Each end of the string should be in a corner of the baulk. (The datum line can be located anywhere on the side of the baulk where there are no projecting stones or bricks that will prevent it from being strung horizontally.) A baulk longer than five metres will probably have to be drawn in two stages, as long strings will sag and make it difficult to keep the datum line horizontal. The technical staff should take the elevation of the two ends of the datum line so that the elevation of the lines in adjacent squares can be correlated. Two line-levels should be placed on the datum line to help keep the line horizontal during the drawing. A cloth metric tape is placed next to the datum line and attached with clothes pegs either on the two end nails or the datum line itself.

At given points, e.g. every twenty-five centimetres, take vertical measurements upwards or downwards from the line to the top of each layer with a metal tape. As one worker takes the measurements along the datum line, a second plots the readings on the graph paper. Gentle layers produce points that can be connected without much difficulty. When a slope changes rapidly between two points, however, the changes must be planned in greater detail. The first layer to plot is the unexcavated surface of the baulk. Next, each layer under the surface in successive order is plotted until you reach the limit of the excavation.

When all the layers have been plotted put the baulk tag numbers in their corresponding position on the section drawing, adding a description of soil colour and texture (see Chapter 7). Finally, sketch all large rocks, bricks, and large artifacts in their respective positions. These details will help to correlate photographs of the baulk with the section drawing.

A section should show all walls as they appear at the point where they enter the baulk, and the upper limits of layers of stone or rubble, foundation trenches, post holes and other features that may be present. You can now compare the section drawing with those of squares adjacent to the baulk, by relating the elevations of the

datum line of each drawing to each other and adjusting the sections so that the surfaces and the layers correspond.

This correlation of layers in the baulk of one square, or between a series of squares, is a preliminary step to determining the sequence of past events. Figure 8.2 is an illustration of a simplified one-period site, that is, a site that has but one historical period represented in both the architecture and artifacts recovered from the soil and debris layers associated with the architecture. The historical period may be short or long, but there is usually a continuous use of the site during that time. A period has one or more *phases*, each phase being an observable combination of layers in the section that represents a definite historical entity. A phase may be one or more layers with their associated architecture, called an architectural phase, or a series of layers associated with the abandonment prior to or after an architectural phase, called a phase of abandonment. In figure 8.2 the section shows four phases: a pre-building phase (layers 10 to 12), a phase associated with the use of the building (layers 5-9 & wall A), and two phases of abandonment, the first of collapse (layers 3 and 4) and the second a post-building phase (layers 2 and 1).

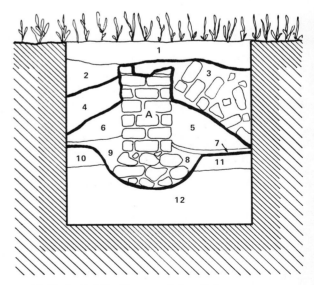

| 10-12 | Pre-Building Phase | 3-4 | Collapse |
| 5-9 | Phase of Occupation | 1-2 | Post-Building Phase |

Figure 8.2. A section showing the history of a wall in a one-period site.

Do the "phasing" of every section during the field season, as it requires the cooperation of the director and area supervisors at the site. It is not sufficient to phase the sections of each square independently of the sections from contiguous squares, as the total result must be a coherent picture of the entire site at each stage of its history. At complex sites the director will want to prepare plans for each architectural period, and possibly for each phase of the periods as well. This can only be done if the sections are phased when drawn.

A finished field section drawing should include a summary statement, usually presented in the form of a chart, indicating the various periods and phases, and the architecture and layers associated with each.

Photograph each baulk both in black and white and colour, to show what it actually looked like at the time the section was drawn. The photographs of the baulks augment and verify the section drawings, which are necessarily the results of interpretation by those who made them. The roll and frame number of all applicable photographs should appear on the section drawing.

As with plans, label section drawings with the site, date, scale, area, square, a description of the baulk being drawn, and the names of the recorders. The completed drawings and photograph record should contain sufficient detail to answer all questions about the stratigraphy of the site. Keep finished drawings in the field laboratory.

ARCHAEOLOGICAL PHOTOGRAPHY

Photography, like other tasks on a dig, requires skill and patience. The photographer has to work under conditions that may not produce the best results. He needs all his professional skill to overcome the limitations imposed on him by the archaeological environment and turn out clear, well composed and detailed photographs.

To learn the qualities of good archaeological photography there is no substitute for experience on a number of digs. A basic knowledge of archaeological techniques, a clearly estab-

lished routine for daily photography work, and the assistance of area supervisors also make the photographer's task easier. He should observe the site under varying light conditions and take advantage of the best opportunities to bring out the different texture of soils and rocks so tone differences in layers will show up well on black and white photographs.

The importance of cleanliness in the square cannot be overemphasized. A messy site detracts from the photographer's work and produces poor pictures for publication. Untrimmed grass on the edges of the baulk, and poor cleaning of the walls and earth features are evident. Lastly, if the dump is too close to the edge of the square it gives the impression of a careless operation. Such photographs tell the viewer more about the archaeological techniques and standards of excavation than they do about the results they are meant to record.

Photographs are taken at every important step in the removal of layers and features of archaeological significance from each square. All important objects are photographed in position before they are removed, to show the location and extent of pits, post holes, foundation trenches of former walls, drip lines from the eaves of buildings, etc. To complement the section drawings photographs of the sides of the four principal baulks and all subsidiary baulks, probe trenches and test pits are necessary. When vandalism is a problem you may have to photograph the square at the end of each day's work so that any disturbances can be noted and recorded.

The Camera and Accessories

There are a number of good cameras to choose from in equipping a dig. The make you buy will depend in part on the amount of money available for photography equipment. The 35mm single reflex camera is the basic unit for field photography, although some archaeologists prefer to have a camera that makes a negative, anywhere from 8 x 10 inches down to 2 ¼ x 2 ¼ inches. A Bronica or Hasselblad roll film camera produces excellent pictures, but are, unfortunately, expensive. If the budget permits, get two 35mm cameras, one for black and white photography and the second for coloured slides, or one 35mm camera for coloured slides and a 2 ¼ x 2 ¼ inch, or larger negative camera for black and white photos.

The Asahi Pentax SP 1000 has been used by the authors on historical archaeological digs in Canada with consistently good performance. Alternative cameras would be the Nikon, Nikkormat, or Canon TX, all of which have performed well in archaeological work in different parts of the world.

A selection of three lenses is usually adequate for most archaeological work. These include:

1. A wide-angle (short focal length) lens (28mm f/2.8) for photography where the working distance from the subject is restricted.

2. A normal (medium focal length) lens (55mm f/2) for most situations encountered on a dig. This lens comes as standard equipment with most 35mm single lens reflex cameras.

3. A telephoto (long focal length) lens (135 - 200mm f/3.5) for photographing distant objects. Another important use of telephoto lenses is the isolation of the subject from the background by using a large aperture, thus decreasing the depth of field.

Since lenses are often not interchangeable between different makes, be sure that compatible lenses are available for the camera to be used. The photographer will also need lens covers, a sturdy tripod, cable release, filters, and a camera case.

Lens covers should be used on the back and front of all lens units to prevent damage from dirt and dust. Lenses are expensive; using covers can reduce the cost of maintenance and replacement of camera equipment.

A heavy-duty aluminum tripod is essential, to prevent small hand movements from blurring pictures. Movement of the camera can also be prevented by using a cable release to depress the shutter release button while the camera is mounted on a tripod. A tripod and cable release are especially important on sites where strong winds make a heavy tripod the only way to keep a camera from moving. Even at speeds of 1/250 sec. slight movements can result in blurring detectable on large prints. If possible, the tripod should have adjustable legs with a cross-brace

between the three, and should be extendable to a height of two metres or more from the ground. It should be possible to tilt the head of the tripod 90 degrees downward or upward for vertical photography.

Store camera equipment in a sturdy, dust-proof case, with a shoulder strap and sufficient space for lenses, filters, film, a second camera body, and small distance scales. You can usually buy a second-hand camera case at a fraction of the cost of a new one. Dust-proof suitcases can be used as camera cases by filling them with foam rubber and cutting out holes to fit the equipment. Such a suitcase has the advantage of showing the photographer at a glance exactly what is there and what is missing.

FILTERS

Filters are useful in black and white photography because they increase the contrast between different parts of the subject that would otherwise have similar or identical tone value on a print. The filters most useful on a dig are red, green and light yellow.

Filters transmit the colour of the filter while absorbing others. A red filter will absorb blue or green colours; a green filter will absorb red and blue; while a yellow filter will absorb blue but allow most other colours to be transmitted. On a black and white print a filter lightens the tone of objects its own colour and darkens the tone of colours it absorbs. The more intense the colour of the filter, the stronger the contrast it produces. The general rule is to choose a filter the same as the colour you want lightest in the photograph.

Since the action of filters is to absorb light and cut down the total amount striking the film, the exposure length must be increased to compensate for the filter's effect. A guide to filter factors is usually included with the purchase of a filter. The effect of a filter can be determined by viewing a subject through it and noting the changes in contrast that occur. For example, a red filter will darken the sky in a photograph. Here experience in the use of filters is the best asset for good results. When the correct filter is chosen it should be mounted on the camera before the camera is focused.

All lenses should have an ultra-violet filter on them. This holds back ultra-violet rays and limits the amount of haze in photographs. This filter also protects the outer lens element and should a filter get scratched it is less expensive to replace than to have a lens reground. There is no filter factor for an ultra-violet filter.

Filters should be purchased after the lenses, as different size filters are available and should the size of the filter be different from the front of the lens, a series of ring adapters will be needed. Filters usually come in a plastic case to prevent scratching and dirt from entering. It is a good practice to store filters in their cases, as a damaged filter will affect the quality of photographs with which it is used.

Many 35mm cameras are equipped with through-the-lens light meters and do not need to be adjusted for filter factor. If a camera does not have a built-in light meter, a standard light meter such as the Gossen Lunasix will serve most archaeological needs.

FILM

The photographer must keep in mind a number of things when considering the type of film to buy. First, if the camera equipment to be used is not his own, he should check to make sure of the film size needed, 35mm, 120mm, etc. Second, he should be sufficiently familiar with the site to know what lighting problems he is likely to encounter. This will help him to determine what ASA film he should use. The ASA (American Standards Association) number of a film expresses the light sensitivity of the film. The numbers vary from as low as 15 all the way to 3,000. The lower the number the less sensitive the film. Conversely, the lower the number the more light one needs to take a picture, or the higher the ASA the less light one needs. The higher the ASA the grainier the film; it is important to remember this as you consider such things as the use of photographs for enlargements. For example, if a high ASA film such as Tri-X (ASA 400) is used, then an enlargement to 8 x 10 inches will show a definite grain; whereas if a low ASA film such as Panatomic-X, (ASA 32) is used, an enlargement from a 35mm negative can be made to well over 40 x 60 inches without any grain showing. The two examples given above

are both black and white films. A black and white film such as Kodak Plus-X or Ilford FP 4, both with ASA 125, are a good compromise between a low ASA film and a high one. Should lighting conditions be poor, as happens indoors or in extreme shade, then a high speed film should be used. The same holds true for colour films. Kodachrome is a good slide film and makes good black and white prints from coloured slides. Alternative colour films are Kodak Ektachrome or Agfachrome.

There are a number of good commercial films that an archaeologist can use in field work. The choice of brands is a matter of preference and proximity to a source of supply during the dig.

Field Techniques

SCALES, BOARDS AND STRINGS

To give the viewer an idea of the size of the subject, all photographs should include an accurate scale, graduated in metres or centimetres. You can make one of 1x1-inch seasoned hardwood. For black and white photographs paint it in alternate divisions of black and white; for coloured photographs, red and yellow. (Chipped or dirty scales can spoil a photograph; paint them freshly at the beginning of each season.)

The length of the scale depends on the size of the subject. An object in the soil, for example, requires a scale of 5 or 10 centimetres only. A view of a deep trench requires a 1-metre scale, while a general view of the entire site may demand a 2-metre pole, photographed at one or more positions to indicate the height of background features.

The scale should be as unobtrusive as possible. Place it vertically or horizontally depending on the subject and the plane one is most likely to want to measure - vertical for heights of walls, for example, and horizontal for widths. The scale should always be parallel and near to the edge of a photograph, so that it can be cropped out of prints where it is not needed.

For photographs of large areas a human figure can be used as an approximate scale. (Make sure the model is busy at work rather than staring stiffly and ominously at the camera.) Diggers are usually willing to allow their photographs to be used in reports and publicity; for other uses it is a courtesy to ask the model's permission. The intended use of the shot and the agreed terms under which it is used should be put down in writing.

Some excavators regularly include a small board with moveable plastic letters and numbers in photographs, to label all shots. Although this eliminates the chance of mislabelling negatives and prints in the laboratory, it does mean a prominent distraction from the subject of the photograph. Photographs to be used in published reports should not have boards in them. In the same way, the presence of baulk strings distracts the viewer from the subject and results in poor composition. Archaeologists do not agree on whether strings should be kept in photographs or not, as it is to some extent a matter of taste, but the authors have always found it best to remove the strings for final photographs of a layer or feature. If each square has been strung separately, it will be an easy matter to unwind the string from the corner nails or pegs and place it temporarily out of sight.

UNDERCUTTING SOIL LAYERS

When two successive layers are of the same or similar colour and texture some archaeologists will undercut the upper layer to form a shadow over the second layer, thus increasing the definition between them on a photograph. This practice negates the purpose of the photography - to make a visual record of the baulks and features *as they are*, and not as the excavator interprets them. Filters can be used as a substitute for undercutting, as the filter can provide the contrast that is sought without marking the baulk.

RE-TOUCHING NEGATIVES

For the same reason, the archaeological negatives should not be re-touched or manipulated in any way that could be construed as an alteration of the evidence being recorded. If there is any fear that the tone contrasts will be inadequate, it is much better to take several shots of a section, each under a different light condition, than to re-touch the negatives afterwards. The practice of "bracketing a shot" can also be used where lighting conditions are difficult. Take

three pictures of the same thing, first one as the meter indicates (e.g. f11 at 1/125) then a second on the low side (f8 at 1/125), and finally, one on the high side (f16 at 1/125). This ensures good contrast in at least one of the three shots.

WETTING LAYERS

One technique to bring out tone contrasts between soil layers and architectural features is to wet a section before photography. A sand and pebble layer, for instance, will dry more rapidly than a clay or loam layer, and the difference in tone between wet and dry layers will provide the necessary contrast for a photograph. In locations where heavy morning dews occur the moisture may be provided naturally; otherwise, wet the surface of the subject evenly with a small hand sprayer. It is a good practice to photograph the same baulk wet and then dry in order to have a set of pictures for comparative study.

THE PHOTOGRAPH REGISTER

A large number of photographs are taken during an excavation; it is essential to keep a complete record for sorting out the negatives and for checking to make sure that all necessary photographs have been taken before the site is filled in.

These are the essential parts of a photograph register sheet:

Camera and Film Type

Since at any one time you may be using a number of makes of camera and film, it is important to record the camera name or number and film type for each roll. This will help identify, if necessary, a faulty camera or a bad lot of film.

Roll Number

All rolls of film should be numbered consecutively beginning with the number one. If a dig lasts more than one season, the second season's film should also be numbered consecutively, beginning after the last number of the previous season. Numbering film helps to maintain an inventory of photographs and provides a cross-reference with the photograph register and excavation record forms.

Exposure Number

This is a sequential number that should correspond to the number of frames on the film. If an exposure is to be omitted, this should be indicated on the register sheet.

Date

Enter the date on the form by using numerals for the day followed by the month. The first of August, for instance, would be written 1/8.

Exposure

The shutter opening and speed should be recorded. Although this will be no use after the film has been exposed, it will help the photographer analyze and improve his work.

Description of Subject

Include space in the register for a description of the subject of each photograph, (especially square and layer or feature) the reason for the photograph, and the compass direction in which the photograph is taken.

Initials of Photographer

The initials of the photographer are useful when more than one person is doing field work. The director may want to discuss photographic details with the cameraman and to credit correctly photos used in publication, etc.

Once the dig film has been processed the register is a guide to cataloguing the negatives and a help in locating all photographic records after the dig is ended.

THE DARK ROOM

If a photographer is experienced in running a dark room and if there are adequate facilities for developing black and white film, it helps to process the film as it is taken. This practice will eliminate a lot of the uncertainty that inevitably arises when the quality of photographic coverage cannot be determined before layers or features are removed from the square. However, an on-site dark room is not always possible; it requires a clean water supply, electricity, a clean room for work, and a room, large enough to work in, from which light can be completely blocked. If a dig is near a town you can probably arrange for a local photographer to process the film almost as fast as it can be done on the site. In a more remote area an on-site dark room may be more important. The decision to set it up will depend on whether the photographer is skilled in processing film and whether his own schedule and the dig facilities make it feasible.

Chapter 9

THE COLLECTION AND CARE OF ARTIFACTS AND SAMPLES

An artifact deposited in the ground deteriorates until it has established an equilibrium with its surroundings, at which time the rate of deterioration reaches a minimum. The rate of deterioration and ultimate condition of an artifact will depend on its chemical composition and physical structure, the environment in which it is enclosed, and the seasonal fluctuations in temperature and moisture to which it is exposed. For example, a piece of iron in a moist temperate climate will deteriorate to a greater extent than one deposited an equal length of time in a desert. By the time equilibrium is established between the artifact and its environment it may have deteriorated to such an extent that it is unidentifiable and of little help to the historical archaeologist. In some environments, on the other hand, the artifact may be preserved in mint condition.

When an artifact is uncovered the established equilibrium is destroyed and deterioration accelerated. The conservation technician must understand the effects of exposure to the atmosphere (oxygen, moisture and heat) on different material, and be prepared to employ suitable methods to counteract them. Such methods may involve either maintaining the old environment or compensating for the new one through special treatments.

After an artifact has been uncovered it must be carefully removed from the soil, prepared, and packaged to prevent any deterioration beyond what may have already occurred. The field archaeologist's ability to collect and care for artifacts is crucial if they are to survive any prolonged delay from the time of discovery to the time of study and examination.

A small but well equipped field conservation laboratory should be part of the technical facilities at every dig. Its equipment and lay-out should be established before excavation starts, so that supervisory staff can see where and how the conservation work will be carried out. Also, the director should consult a trained conservator beforehand to anticipate and prepare for problems. Such a person will be able to give good advice about the types of artifacts likely to be found at the site.

Ideally, every excavation should have a trained conservator on its technical staff, to supervise the lifting of artifacts and their subsequent treatment and packaging. This is rarely possible, except on a very large excavation, because of the expense and the critical shortage of trained conservators in Canada. When a trained conservator is not available, the best arrangement is to designate one person to be responsible for field conservation. A week or two of introductory training in a museum's conservation department should prepare him for the kind of first aid required by artifacts in the field. Failing this, the director will have to train a conservation technician in the essential techniques. This technician should handle the job all through the dig, not only to minimize demands on the director for instruction, but also to guarantee that the same standard of care is given to all materials.

That one person is designated conservation technician does not mean that the other crew members need not be knowledgeable or concerned. The conservation technician will not be able to supervise the uncovering of every artifact, and the area supervisor and other mem-

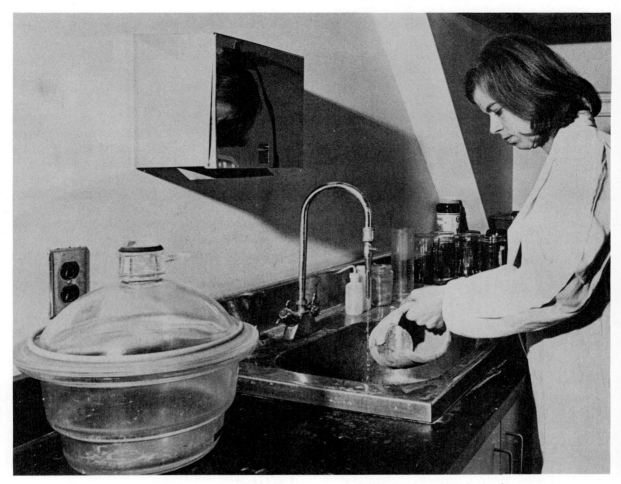

Plate 9.1. A technician washing pottery in the lab. In the foreground can be seen a dessicator, used for impregnating porous pottery in order to strengthen it. Adequate water pressure is necessary to operate the dessicator.

bers of the excavation crew will frequently have to decide whether special treatment will be necessary before removing artifacts.

Since you will probably have neither a trained conservator nor all the equipment necessary for permanent conservation of artifacts, do not attempt any field conservation other than what is required to get the artifacts safely to a trained conservator. In addition, no treatment applied in the field should be irreversible, as this will hamper the conservation work that will be necessary when the materials arrive at the permanent laboratory. The basic elements of field conservation include special methods for the consolidation, lifting, and protection of artifacts removed from the ground, and the packaging and labelling of artifacts for transport. The techniques outlined in this chapter are intended for field reference only, and are not meant to be a complete guide to conservation methods.

CONSOLIDATING AND REMOVING ARTIFACTS FROM THE GROUND

If possible, examine each artifact before it is removed from its place of discovery to determine whether or not it can be safely lifted and placed

Plate 9.2. A small iron pot before (left) and after (right) being treated by a trained conservator.

in an artifact bucket. If the artifact appears to be structurally weak and there is a possibility of damage during removal, you will have to strengthen (i.e. consolidate) it before it is lifted. An adhesive substance such as a resin or a wax is an economical and versatile consolidant. The usual field procedure is to coat an artifact (using a small brush or garden sprayer) with a consolidant until a protective skin is formed, making the originally fragile artifact a structurally strong unit.

The type of resin or wax to use will depend on the type of material encountered. The consolidants found to be most versatile and valuable on historical archaeology excavations are polyvinyl acetate (PVA) and polyethylene glycol (PEG).

Polyvinyl Acetate (PVA V15)

This is a crystalline substance soluble in ethanol. A concentration of 10 per cent to 15 per cent PVA should be prepared for most field work, although the exact concentration will depend on the material being consolidated. Practical experience should help to determine the concentration appropriate for each situation. Use PVA in a well ventilated area and store it in a closed container. PVA is available in Canada from the British Drug House, Toronto.

Polyethylene Glycol (PEG)

This substance is available under the name of Carbowax. Carbowax 4000 is an all-purpose, water-soluble consolidant especially useful for treating wood in either wet or dry conditions. Polyethylene glycol is available in Canada from Union Carbide (Canada) Ltd., Toronto.

Lifting

If an artifact or object is not structurally strong enough to be removed by careful lifting, sliding onto a flat board, or by applying a consolidant, then you will have to encase it in plaster of Paris.

Plaster of Paris (gypsum plaster) can be obtained from most hobby shops and should be prepared according to the instructions which accompany each package. The advantages of plaster of Paris over other lifting substances such as polyurethane foam are its cheapness and availability. Its disadvantages are its heaviness and the fact that when it hardens it is chemically irreversible and may damage the surface of artifacts. The reversibility of all treatments being a basic principle of field conservation plaster should not be applied directly to an artifact but separated from it by a protective barrier of damp paper, polyethylene, or plastic wrap. The plaster can be placed over this protective barrier to encase the artifact. When the plaster has hardened, the enclosed artifact can be safely lifted.

Containers and Packing Material

To prevent damage when moving artifacts from the excavation to the field laboratory or from the field laboratory to the permanent laboratory, proper containers and packing materials should be supplied to the excavation and technical crews. Since the sizes of artifacts and objects can be expected to range from that of a sewing needle or small pewter button to that of a large storage crock, several different size containers will be needed. Small paper or plastic boxes are useful for holding small artifacts. Three convenient sizes are 2x3x1 inch; 5½x4x1½ inch; and 8x5½x3 inch. These can be packed into larger corrugated cartons for transport to the permanent laboratory. If small paper boxes have to be made in specific sizes by a box manufacturer, you will have to purchase a minimum number, which may be sufficient for several digs. Clear plastic boxes with hinged lids have the added advantage of letting you see the contents without unsealing each container.

After lifting large artifacts from the squares, place them in double-thickness corrugated cartons. (Used cartons are available from food and department stores.) Polyethylene (plastic) and paper bags can be used for packaging dry (never wet or damp) artifacts. Paper bags varying in sizes from small candy bags to large shopping bags should be available. Plastic bags should be of heavy gauge (500 gauge) thickness and of a variety of sizes up to 18x24 inches. Although the plastic bags allow you to see the contents without opening them, they have the disadvantage of holding moisture contained in an artifact, even though it may appear dry. This moisture may cause the growth of moulds and corrosion. If you use plastic bags, add to each one a small packet of silica gel to maintain an even dry atmosphere. If silica gel is not available use paper bags only. Silica gel can be purchased from any scientific supply house.

The most versatile packing materials are acid-free tissue paper, cotton wool, styrofoam, and "bubble-pack". Acid-free tissue paper and cot-

Plate 9.3. Washing pottery in the field laboratory.

ton wool are inexpensive and can be obtained from most packing companies. Cotton wool is also available in one pound rolls from local pharmacists. Never put cotton wool in contact with an artifact, however, as it may become intertwined with and dislodge any fragile surfaces it touches. Wrap a piece of tissue paper around the cotton wool as a protective layer between the wool and the artifact. Styrofoam and bubble pack are available from packaging companies in larger cities, but are more expensive than tissue paper or cotton wool.

Labelling

The excavation crew should label each artifact box or bag with its origin, identification, and details about any materials and treatment which has been applied during either the consolidation, lifting, or packaging of the contents. This information will be an invaluable guide to the field laboratory staff and later to the trained conservator, who wants to know what measures have been taken to protect the artifact, as well as any precautions that should be taken during unpacking. Every artifact that is to be handled as an "object" (see chaper 8) should have been noted in the object register and given an object number. This will mean that each box or bag will have to be examined and the object handled again before being sent to the trained conservator. To minimize handling, place a list of the contents of each carton on the outside and

Plate 9.4. *Checking artifact bucket tags with the register before packing and shipping objects to the permanent laboratory.*

enclose a duplicate hand-written or typed copy in the carton. On the outside of all cartons should be a large arrow to indicate which side is up and which side to open. Cartons should be sealed with paper or cloth tape, and secured with metal bands or heavy twine. Pack very heavy objects in wooden crates.

Field Treatment of Various Materials

The exact procedure for lifting and packaging of an artifact will depend on the material and its condition when uncovered. The following paragraphs will introduce field conservation procedures for the more common materials found at an historical site.

IRON

Artifacts commonly made of iron include nails, axe heads, chisels, tools, keys, heel taps, buttons and heating stoves. The treatment of iron artifacts depends on their size and condition. Small dry ones should be kept dry; washing will only accelerate deterioration. Each should be placed in a paper or plastic box just large enough to hold it. Line the container with paper, place the artifact on a pad of cotton wool covered with tissue paper, and place another pad on top. Closing the lid should pack the artifact firmly in the container. A small quantity of silica gel should be placed in the container to equalize moisture. A number of boxes can be packed in a larger carton, the carton closed with tape, and then placed inside a large polyethylene bag. This bag should be sealed, with a small quantity of silica gel enclosed.

Large iron artifacts found in a dry condition should be placed in a large, padded cardboard carton with a quantity of silica gel. It is important that a large artifact be properly supported and held firmly in the carton to prevent damage in transit.

Iron artifacts found wet, regardless of size, should be kept wet until treated by a trained conservator. To pack them, line a cardboard carton or wooden crate (for very heavy things) with a polyethylene bag. Place one or more artifacts in the bag and fill it with water enough to cover them. Each artifact will have to have an identifying tag written in indelible ink. Add a solution of fungicide, such as a 1 per cent solution of Dowicide G, to the water. (Dowicide G is available in Canada from the Dow Chemical Company, Toronto.) Dowicide G powder should be mixed in a well ventilated room. The container should be examined regularly during any prolonged storage to check for leakage or evaporation.

BRONZE

Bronze artifacts such as keys and buttons should be handled with care, especially when the surface is covered with a thin green layer of corrosion. In such cases the original surface of the metal may be within rather than underneath the corrosion. To avoid damaging it do not wash or scrub the artifact. Bronze can be stored in the same way as iron, but should be inspected regularly for bright green spots or corrosion. If corrosion starts again, replace the silica gel in the container. Wet bronze artifacts should not be stored in water, but allowed to dry slowly and then stored in dry conditions.

SILVER

Artifacts of silver, such as cutlery or candle holders, are often found corroded with dirty brown silver chloride. Silver artifacts are easily damaged and therefore should not be cleaned at the site but packed dry in paper or plastic boxes between pads of tissue paper and sent to a trained conservator. Do not pack silver so tightly in a box that undue pressure is put on it.

LEAD, PEWTER AND TIN

Avoid washing or scrubbing these metals as they crack easily if very thin or brittle. Pack them in acid-free tissue paper and put them in plastic bags. Avoid paper boxes, as the paper will speed up the rate of corrosion of lead alloys. If a pewter or tin artifact is in a very fragile condition it should be taken immediately to a trained conservator.

GLASS

Glass artifacts rarely present any serious problem in the field, other than the need to protect them from breaking. Wet glass should be dried slowly and packed between pads of tissue paper. A number of glass artifacts from the same layer, such as window glass or bottle fragments, can be individually registered and packed together in the same container between alternate layers of tissue paper.

If there is reason to believe that wet glass is unstable and will be damaged or seriously discoloured if dried, then it should be photographed and packed in wet tissue paper. A carton of glass artifacts should be enclosed in a heavy gauge polyethylene bag to retain the moisture. A little fungicide sprayed on the packing will help retard the growth of mould.

POTTERY

If a pot is fragmented it can be held together by coating it with a 5 per cent solution of polyvinyl acetate dissolved in ethanol. Remove the pot after the consolidant has dried, and place it in a box padded with tissue paper. All other pottery sherds are hard enough to be washed in clear water without damage. The only exception to this rule are sherds that show flaking glaze and those that have been painted or slipped. These should not be washed, as the slip and glaze will be damaged by scrubbing.

If sherds are mended on the site, be sure the edges are clean. Begin by coating the edges of the sherd with 5 per cent PVA. Then use Ambroid adhesive to join them, and a box of clean, white sand (available at most builders' supply stores) to support the joined sherds until the adhesive has dried. (Ambroid is available at hardware and hobby supply stores.) Masking tape can be used to hold sherds together until the adhesive has set, but should not be put on a fragile surface, as it might dislodge the glaze or applied decoration. If an adhesive other than Ambroid is used on a pot, record this information on the artifact card.

WOOD

Wet wood, if allowed to dry for any period of time, will crack and be permanently damaged. To avoid this, keep it wet at all times. This can be done by periodic spraying with a garden sprayer or hose. Covering the wood with dark polyethylene will help keep moisture in. Large wooden objects such as floor beams are more difficult to.lift because of their size and need to be kept wet during the lifting. The beam should be wrapped in·a large sheet of polyethylene and sealed to prevent the loss of moisture. It may be necessary to support weak wooden beams on long boards covered with foam rubber. A small amount of fungicide should be sprayed on the wood.

Wood should be stored in tanks of water when it arrives at the permanent laboratory. Stored wood should be checked from time to time for evidence of drying or fungus growth.

If a wooden floor or other structure is to be saved, it will have to be dismantled into separate units and each of these wrapped. Do this after the structure has been photographed and drawn *in situ* for the excavation records.

LEATHER

Leather is found on historical sites in shoes and straps, and should be maintained in the same state in which it is found. If the leather is wet pack it wet, sprayed with a fungicide solution. This will prevent brittleness and cracking. If the leather is dry then it should be padded in tissue paper and kept dry until it can be properly conserved. If leather needs to be consolidated before being lifted use PEG 1500 applied with a brush or the fingers.

BONE AND IVORY

Animal bone can be washed and left to dry before packing. If it needs to be consolidated, use a 5 per cent PVA solution in ethanol. Artifacts such as buttons, handles on cutlery and brushes, and combs should be left unwashed, especially if it is not possible to distinguish bone from ivory. If ivory is wet when uncovered, keep it in this condition in a plastic bag, and use a fungicide solution to control the growth of mould. Ivory should never be washed but cleaned mechanically before packing.

STONE

Stone objects should be washed in clear water and allowed to dry slowly to prevent crystallization of soluble salts as moisture is removed. After the stone is dry, pack it in boxes with silica gel.

For treatment of materials not mentioned here, a conservation technician should have available a few of the many up-to-date books on conservation techniques. Standard reference books on conservation are listed in the bibliography for this chapter.

THE CARE OF ARTIFACTS IN THE FIELD LABORATORY

Materials brought into the field laboratory each day will be of three categories: (1) artifacts in artifact buckets; (2) objects which have been lifted and packed in boxes or bags without any special treatment; and (3) objects in boxes or bags that have been treated and packed by the field conservator or under his supervision. The materials in categories (1) and (2) may be processed in the field laboratory if you have the staff and facilities. Materials in category (3) should be processed only through step one following, and then packed and transported to a professional conservator for further work. These are the procedures used in processing artifacts in the field laboratory:

Checking Artifact Buckets and Objects

When the artifact buckets are delivered to the field laboratory check the information on the tags, boxes, and bags for completeness, accuracy and legibility. The artifact bucket register and object register should also be checked to ensure that the bucket numbers and other information are properly entered. All bucket tags and register pages should be written with indelible ink so that if they become damp they will remain legible.

The conservation technician should go through the artifact bucket and select any of the artifacts that should be designated objects. Even though the field crew will have selected some objects from their artifact material, there may be more.

When objects are placed in separate boxes their origin, identification and information about any treatment they have received should be written on the lid and on the side of the lower half of the box. This will allow the correct lid and bottom to be matched if the two become separated.

Cleaning the Artifacts

When cleaning any artifact assume it is fragile. Sort out the artifacts and objects that can be safely washed and those that should be cleaned with a soft bristle or nylon brush. Artifacts should be thoroughly dried before they are registered and packed. Paper egg cartons or egg dividers make convenient (and inexpensive) drying trays. Further information on cleaning artifacts has been given in previous sections of this chapter.

Not all digs will have facilities for a washing station. A supply of fresh, clean water and sufficient staff are necessary to do field washing and other possible work such as the code marking of sherds and reconstruction.

Registering Artifacts

Once cleaned, an artifact should be registered and marked with a code showing its origin and register number. Registering artifacts is a tedious job, requiring great care to ensure that the letters and numbers are legible and yet as small as possible. The artifact numbers should be placed on the least conspicuous surface so that they will not show if the artifacts are photographed or displayed. For the sake of those analyzing the

sherds, though, make the markings easy to locate, by placing them in the same general position on all artifacts of the same type. Registration numbers should not be marked on edges that might later be joined together during reconstruction. Write the registration information in India ink and cover it with a thin coat of Incralac or PVA to prevent it being washed or rubbed off. On a porous surface apply an undercoat of Incralac before lettering to prevent the ink from bleeding into the body of the artifact.

If an artifact is too small, or for other reasons the registration cannot be entered directly on its surface, use a jewellery tag that can be attached to it. Depending on the nature and quantity of material being processed, it may not be necessary to register every artifact. For example, at a pottery site there may be more than twenty-five thousand sherds retrieved in a month-long excavation. Some will be badly chipped, or too small to yield any specific information on the vessel's form, glaze, or manufacturing method. In these situations only the sherds that will yield information on pottery types (called diagnostic sherds) should be registered, and the remainder placed in a labelled container with the other artifacts from the bucket. Diagnostic sherds for pottery are usually rims, handles, spouts, bases and decorated sherds from the body of the vessel. The unregistered sherds are useful in reconstructing the forms shown by the diagnostic sherds. If, in the process of labelling, you discover that two or more sherds can be joined, they can be temporarily attached with masking tape. Only one of them should be registered.

Preparing the Artifact Card

Detailed information about each registered artifact or object is entered on a specially prepared card called an artifact card. This information will enable the archaeologist to study the material without having to handle the artifacts at each stage of research. Information should be entered on the card when the artifact is being registered, to be updated as necessary. The design of the card will differ according to the kinds of artifacts to be expected at an excavation, and you may want to prepare specific cards for each. These may be reproduced in quantity

(a)△   (b)▽

Plate 9.5. Mending a lid: (a) finding the exact join spot between two fragments; (b) glu-
ing the join; (c) once the join has been glued it is held in place using small strips of masking tape; and (d) placed in a sandbox until the adhesive has set.

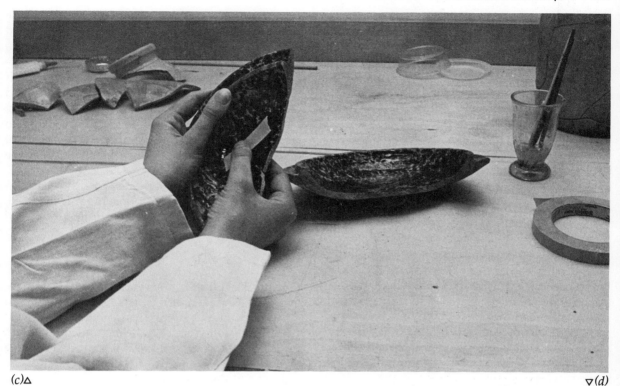

(c)△   ▽(d)

Plate 9.5 continued

without great expense. There should be space for the registration information, a black and white photograph of the artifact, and details of the form, glaze colour, and other descriptive notes. If the object is treated by a conservator the details should be entered. You will also want to indicate the steps through which the artifact is to be taken during processing. The technical description of an artifact should be completed on the site only if a trained artifact analyst is available. He is then the person responsible for deciding what additional processing is necessary.

Reconstruction

A significant percentage of artifacts will join or mend with one or more artifacts from the same or consecutive buckets. After the diagnostic artifacts have been registered, and if there is time, you can spread the material out on tables and attempt to reconstruct it. On all but fragile surfaces, masking tape may be used to hold the joins temporarily. With time, though, masking tape can leave stains or adhesive deposits; do the permanent glueing as soon as the artifact is completely assembled. Partially or completely reconstructed objects should be photographed in the field laboratory in colour and black and white. If an artifact does not reconstruct either draw it as it is, or, in the case of an earthenware pottery sherd, cut it with a diamond-studded lapidary saw so that a cross-section can be drawn rapidly on the reverse side of the artifact card. Sherds that are to be sawed will have to be doubly registered, that is, the registration placed in two places so that both fragments will have a number.

SAMPLING

Historical archaeology can benefit greatly from the cooperation of specialists in other disciplines. Multi-disciplinary studies of environmental evidence from historical sites are providing much new information on the past. Scientists able to help you may be found in museums, universities, or industrial laboratories. Contact them before a dig begins so that you will know what samples to collect during the field season. A collection of material made before a research project has been developed does not generally yield much significant data, and a specialist may want to make his own collections at the site. In this case the field staff should be informed of the impending visit, and work space provided. Occasionally a specialist will ask that collections be made according to specific instructions. In this case the reliability of the collections is the sole responsibility of the director.

Substances usually collected on historical sites include soils and soil sections, organic material, and samples of slag, glaze, or other industrial waste materials.

SOIL

Samples of all soil layers encountered in a square should be taken, for further mechanical and possibly chemical analysis. About one-half pound of soil from each layer is adequate, with the soil taken from a freshly-scraped face of a baulk. The sample from each layer should be dried and then put into a clear polyethylene bag with an appropriate label.

ORGANIC MATERIALS

Organic substances such as wood and charcoal, pollen and seeds, should be collected according to the instructions of a specialist to avoid contamination of the evidence. Organic materials are usually found wet, and should be kept wet and put into a polyethylene bag.

INDUSTRIAL SAMPLES

Samples of slag, glaze, lead oxide from a pottery shop, or other industrial products that are found on a site may be collected for further chemical analysis. A good rule of thumb is to collect at least five times the amount that will ultimately be necessary for the study. If the samples are found wet, let them dry slowly and pack them in polyethylene or paper bags or boxes.

All samples should be accompanied by detailed information on the origin, date, description of contents, collecting methods, and the name of the collector.

Chapter 10

PREPARING THE EXCAVATION REPORT

Your excavation report should be written to appeal to as wide an audience as possible, from the intelligent person with no knowledge of archaeology to the experienced professional. A multitude of details does not mean that a report has to be dull or incomprehensible. Present the information in an orderly and reasoned fashion, each section relevant to what has gone before, and to the general subject under discussion.

Due to increased printing costs, publishers are likely to limit the number of pages devoted to a report in a journal or book. You may have to either abridge the text or select only the more important topics for inclusion in an article to be published. The remainder of the information may have to remain in typescript, deposited where the complete record can be consulted by those with a particular interest in the dig.

When you have chosen an appropriate magazine, journal, or book publisher, it is advisable to contact the editor of the publication to determine whether the subject of the report is of interest to him, and the format in which a manuscript should be submitted. Do this before completing the report, as most journals and magazines require all articles to be submitted according to a specified format and style.

If a report is to be published by an organization with no previous experience in publishing archaeological works, either prepare the manuscript according to a format already in use by a recognized publisher of archaeological works, or according to one of the standard style guides listed in the bibliography to this chapter. When preparing a short report, consult either *Historical Archaeology* (USA), the *Journal of Post-Medieval Archaeology* (Great Britain) or other well established journals in related branches of archaeology for typical examples of an accepted format.

An excavation report contains two types of material: illustrations and text. The illustrations include photographs (called plates) and drawings (called figures). The text includes the written presentation of the evidence of the dig, and an interpretation and discussion of this evidence. General comments on the qualities of a good archaeological photograph have been made in chapter 8. This chapter will discuss the preparation of drawings and the written text.

DRAWINGS

In preparing an archaeological report do not turn away from the use of drawings simply because you feel that they must be done by an artist. It is not works of art you need, but good representations of architectural details, artifacts, maps and sections. Patience, and a basic knowledge of drafting material and tools will help to make your illustrations an important part of the archaeological report.

If possible, the person who has prepared the field drawings should also be responsible for completing the inked drawings. If someone else is to do this then he will have to become intimately familiar with the excavation and the nature of the drawings to be reproduced, visiting the site and examining the structures that are to

Plate 10.1 A well-designed drafting room should have the proper tools and table space and good lighting.

be drawn. Field notes and personal interviews with the area supervisor should also help to answer any questions regarding interpretation of the field drawings that may arise during subsequent preparation of the work.

To achieve good tone contrast a drawing should be kept as clean as possible during preparation. This can be accomplished by maintaining personal cleanliness and periodically cleaning the drawing instruments. Use set squares, T-squares, or even a piece of tissue paper to support the hands and prevent oils from smudging the surface. If a drawing does become smudged it can be cleaned with a powder such as K&E Inking Powder and brushed off. When using a technical pen be careful to avoid using too much powder, and brush thoroughly to prevent clogging the nib.

Tools

THE DRAWING BOARD

Commercial drafting firms offer many different types of drawing board. They vary from simple table models to very expensive floor models costing $400 and more. In buying a drawing board look for a smooth, unwarped surface, solid edges (especially on the sides), and if the board is free-standing, the quality of the legs of the frame and the tilt of the board.

You can make a rugged and reliable drawing board for field work from a rectangular piece of ¾-inch plywood, 24x30 inches in size, with the edges smoothed down with sandpaper. Fasten a piece of wood stripping, ¾x1 inch along the two short sides of the board with glue and finishing

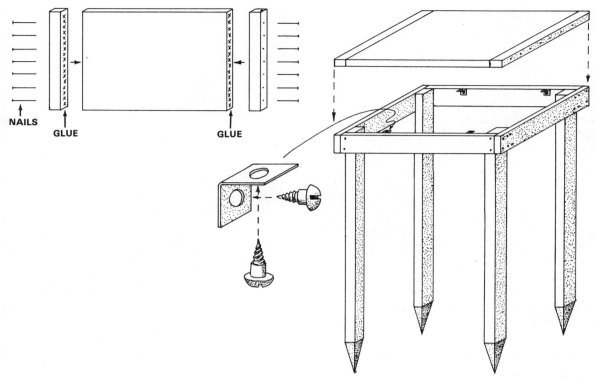

Figure 10.1   Constructing a drafting board.

nails. This trim will give a T-square an even edge
to travel against. Cover the surface of the board
with a drafting vinyl to prevent pitting from the
points of pins or compasses. Drafting vinyl
resembles a thick sheet of hard rubber, green on
one side and cream on the other. It should be
mounted on the board with the green side up.
This colour is easy on the eyes and helps to prevent eyestrain from long hours of work. Drafting vinyl is available from most drafting supply
firms.

T-SQUARE

The T-square is a basic tool for drawing parallel
horizontal lines. It has a straight edge, called the
blade, with a small piece of wood, called the
head, added to the blade at right angles. The
head of the T-square is placed so that it fits
firmly against the sides of the drawing board
and the blade is then moved up and down. As
long as the head of the T-square remains in firm
contact with the board edge, all lines drawn
along the edges of the blade will be parallel to all
other lines drawn along the blade.

Purchase a T-square with the head attached
firmly to the blade by not less than four screws.
This will give greater stability to the head and
prevent any movement of the blade when it is
held firmly against the side of the drawing
board. A second feature to look for is a slight
bevelling of the edge of the blade. This will prevent ink from coming in contact with the blade
and thus smearing the line. Some T-squares provide a plastic strip inserted in the blade edge,
usually slightly raised from the wooden body of
the blade. These T-squares are preferable as they
provide a good guide to rest the pen against, and
are less prone to warping.

SET SQUARES

The set square, when used in conjunction with a
T-square enables the draftsman to draw parallel
vertical lines (see plate 10.3). (A set square is a
triangle, even though it is referred to as a
square.) There are two essential types of set
squares: a 45-degree set square, composed of one
90-degree angle and two angles of 45 degrees
each; and a 30-60-degree set square, composed

Figure 10.2 A T-square is used for drawing parallel, horizontal lines.

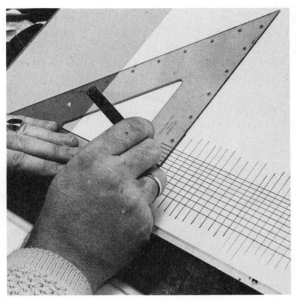

Plate 10.3 The use of a set square in conjunction with a T-square to make parallel vertical lines.

of one 90-degree angle, one angle of 30 degrees and another of 60 degrees. These two set squares when used individually provide the most frequently used angles. By using a combination of these set squares and a T-square, however, it is possible to produce a great variety (see plate 10.4). Buy a set square at least 12 inches along the longest side. Set squares are available in transparent plastic and in different colours, the transparent being the most common although tinted ones are becoming more popular, as they are easier to see against the white surface of the drawing.

DRAFTING PENCILS AND LEADS

The most efficient drafting pencil is the mechanical type with a metal barrel and a set of spring-loaded claws holding the lead. The release button at the end of the barrel allows the lead to be extended to the correct length for a particular task, and permits the use of different grades of lead in one pencil.

The choice of pencil leads depends on the work to be done. When drawing architectural features and artifacts a 4H lead is best, as it gives a smudge-proof line that is relatively easy to erase even from smooth surface paper. Also, the

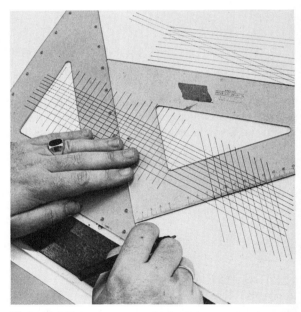

Plate 10.4 Two set squares and a T-square can be used together to produce a variety of angles.

pencil point remains sharp for a longer period of time than with softer leads. A softer lead is recommended for sketching or rendering as it gives greater control over tone. However, softer leads such as 2H will smudge; take care to avoid this when drawing, storing, and transporting finished work. To prevent smudging you can spray drawings with a protective coating, available in aerosol cans from drafting supply houses.

INK AND PENS

When preparing any archaeological drawing it is important that the lines be smooth and of a consistent density of black ink. When ink is used on drafting film, the line density may be too thin, producing a grey appearance especially noticeable on thin lines. This may cause the thin lines to fade out when photographed, yielding an inadequate reproduction. The best contrast is produced by using India ink with a technical pen. A wide selection of pens is available to suit your preferences; the common types available are:

Ruling Pen

This is used for drawing straight lines. The pen consists of a stainless steel shaft separated at one end into two closely-spaced blades. The two blades are drawn together at the tip by means of a screw connecting them together. The distance between the blades determines the line thickness. To use, place a drop of India ink between the two blades and adjust the screw to the desired line thickness. Be careful to keep ink off the outer edges of the blades, as this will make the ink run under the straight edge and smear the finished art work with a blot that will be difficult to remove. After use rinse the pen and clean it gently with a paper towel.

The advantage of the ruling pen is that it will produce almost any line width. Get one that has a click stop on the adjustable screw so that a specific line width can be reproduced whenever desired.

Technical Pen

This pen has now replaced the ruling pen in many drafting offices. It is easier for the beginner to handle and has the added advantage of permitting curved as well as straight lines. The nib consists of a small hollow tube that permits ink to flow down from a reservoir. Inside is a

small plunger with a needle point that acts as a stopper to prevent ink from flowing down the tube when the pen is taken off the drawing surface. Shaking the technical pen will produce a clicking noise, as the plunger moves up and down causing the fine needle point inside the tube to move up and down also. This action starts the flow of ink and cleans the small particles of dried ink out of the tube to permit a smooth flow.

If a technical pen has not been used for a long time it may be necessary to disassemble it for cleaning. When cleaning use extreme care in handling the plunger and wire needle as any bending of the wire will ruin the nib.

Nib sizes are calibrated in different ways depending on the brand. The most common technical pens in Canada are the Koh-i-nor, Leroy and Staedtler-Mars. The nibs of these are calibrated so that the thinnest line available is 0.11 millimetres (6x0) and the thickest is 6.00 millimetres (12). Nibs producing standard line widths are also numbered differently by different manufacturers (see fig. 10.2). You will need a minimum of three nibs for drawing. These should be 00, 1, and 3. If finances permit the purchase of four nibs, then to give a good selection of line thickness the fourth should be size 0.

Straight Pens and Mapping Quills

These are the old-fashioned pens used years ago in Canadian schools. The nib is of a non-reservoir type and is placed in a pen holder. Because there is no reservoir, it is necessary to keep an open bottle of ink by the side of the drawing table. The principal disadvantage of these pens is the fact that they hold relatively little ink and a continuous long line is practically impossible. They cannot be used for drawing lines along a straight edge but are very good for producing ink sketches of a site or an artifact.

SCALES AND GAUGES

A good scale is made of wood with a plastic edge on which the units of measurement are engraved. On the metric scale one edge is calibrated in 1-millimetre and the other in 0.5-millimetre units. The plastic edge and the

line	code	mm.	in.
———————————	6×0	.11	.0045
——————————— —	5×0	.134	.0053
———————————	4×0	19	.0076
———————————	3×0	.25	.0098
———————————	00	.3	.0117
———————————	0	.35	.0138
———————————	1	.46	.018
———————————	2	.56	.022
———————————	$2\frac{1}{2}$	.63	.025
———————————	3	.81	.032
———————————	4	1.14	.045
———————————	6	1.7	.067
———————————	7	2.0	.0787
———————————	8	2.5	.098
———————————	9	3.0	.118
———————————	10	4.0	.158
———————————	11	5.0	.197
———————————	12	6.0	.236

Figure 10.2 The range of nib thicknesses in technical pens. Pens are available by code or line thickness in inches or millimetres. Courtesy Koh-i-noor, Canadian Distributors

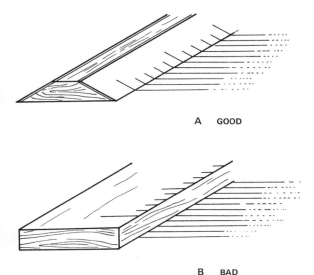

Figure 10.3 Scales should have a bevelled edge (a) to allow the graduations to come as close to the drawing as possible. This prevents parallax as illustrated in (b).

Plate 10.5 Using a Formagage to measure the profile of a pot.

engraved lines of the scale should be arranged so that the units of measurement can be placed directly on the paper. There should be no edge or bevel to prevent the scale from coming in direct contact with the paper. Such a gap makes the scaling of distances less accurate and will create a problem of parallax (see figure 10.3). Do not use a scale to draw straight lines, as this will eventually damage the division markings.

Get a number of scales with different calibrations for drafting work. For some plans and sections the scale of 1:20, or 1:25 may be useful. The number and types of scales needed, however, is determined by the needs of the illustrator.

Calipers

For measuring small artifacts a set of sliding calipers is useful. There are two types: outside and inside. Calipers need not be of the most complicated type, but the span should be at least 10 centimetres, and should allow the illustrator to measure down to .01 centimetres.

Formagage

The Formagage consists of a number of small steel rods held in place by a magnetic holder.

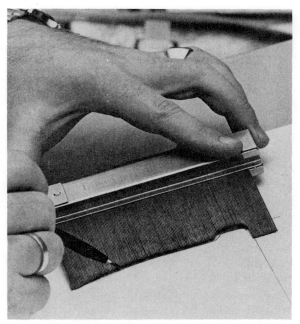

Plate 10.6 Tracing the profile from the Formagage to the drawing paper.

When the ends of the rods are pressed against an uneven surface, such as the side of a pot, the rods will assume the curve of the surface. The rods are then locked into place by a lever on the magnetic holder, and the profile formed by the rods can then be transferred to a drawing. (The Formagage can be purchased from Penn Industries of Philadelphia.)

Materials

Drawing material for the illustrator includes drafting linen, drafting film and tracing paper. For scaled architectural drawings you will need a medium that will not shrink when damp, and has a long storage life, as the drawings are a part of the permanent record of the dig.

DRAFTING LINEN

This is a coated linen treated so as to look and feel like artist's canvas. Although it will not shrink when wet, it is usually used with water-soluble ink that will be damaged. Drafting linen is still used in archaeological work, although it is being replaced by durable and water resistant films.

DRAFTING FILM

Drafting film is a heat-resistant material that is difficult to tear, crease or damage. When unrolled after long storage it will lie flat. The surface is not affected by contact with water or other forms of moisture. Drafting film does not shrink and therefore maintains a constant scale during the lifetime of the drawing. Perhaps the biggest advantage of this material is the fact that extensive mistakes can be easily corrected with a moistened eraser. (To erase unwanted pencil lines on a finished drawing the illustrator should use a soft dry white eraser.)

Drafting films are available in different weights and thicknesses. You will find film of 3 mil (.003-inch) thickness a reliable medium for most archaeological work. The film consists of a tough clear Mylar base to which a translucent drawing surface is applied to one or both sides. Gridded surfaces are available; a non-washout grid will reproduce on a print of the drawing, a washout grid will not. Be sure to specify the kind you want. The least expensive type of drafting film is light-weight, ungridded, with a drawing surface on only one side.

Drafting film is sold under Dietzgen (age-proof) brand and Keuffel & Esser (Herculene)

brand and is available from most drafting supply firms.

TRACING PAPER

Tracing paper is highly translucent and does not yellow with age. You can use both ink and pencil on the paper and erase both repeatedly without damaging the surface. On the other hand it does not store as well as drafting film, it must be kept dry, and it is best stored in a drawing cabinet. Clearprint 1000H tracing paper has been found to be good for general archaeological drawing.

ART BOARD

Art board comes in different colours, thicknesses and textures. For archaeological illustrations a pure white board photographs well and offers the greatest contrast with black ink. Two-ply Strathmore drawing board gives the best combination of weight, surface texture, and durability. This board is particularly useful for drawing artifacts, especially if the field work is to be reproduced photographically without re-drawing. Two-ply Strathmore drawing board has a very smooth surface, takes ink well, and therefore is ideally suited for stippling and extremely fine line work. Its main disadvantage is that it is almost totally opaque and therefore impossible to use for tracing. If you want to trace onto this material use one-ply Strathmore drawing board and place it over a table with a light in it. A fair amount of detail will then show through the board.

A rigid board that is white on one side and untreated on the other is used as a backing for finished art work for photography. Hi-Art 27, available in a number of sizes, is useful for this purpose. The largest size generally stocked in art stores is 30x40 inches, big enough to mount drawings at their full size and still reducible to one-quarter of the original.

STENCILS AND TRANSFERS

These can make lettering and drawing much easier. Lettering can be done with stencils or dry-transfer appliqués. Stencils are clear plastic templates which provide the outlines of letters and numbers. Dry-transfer lettering is becoming popular because it is possible to purchase any number of type faces and sizes on plastic sheets.

Position the required letter or number on the sheet on the drawing and rub it with a ballpoint pen until it is transferred to the drawing. Repeat this procedure for each letter or number, then burnish or rub them to ensure that they are attached to the drawing. Finally, spray the finished work with a protective coating to prevent damage to the lettering. Dry-transfer lettering gives a professional look that otherwise could be achieved only by a skilled hand-letterer. Catalogues listing dry-transfer aids are available free from drafting supply firms.

DRY-TRANSFER PATTERNS

If one area on a drawing is to be set apart from another area, cross-hatching or toning will produce the necessary effect. You can buy transparent plastic sheets with pre-printed self-adhesive patterns in a wide range of symbols

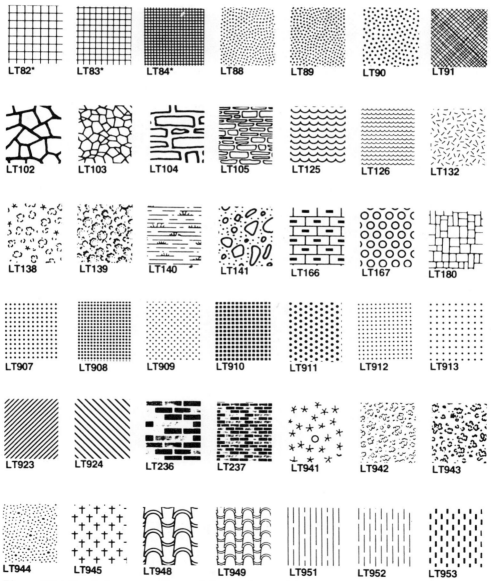

Figure 10.4 Symbols commonly used for sections, plans and maps are available in dry transfer lettering. Courtesy Letraset © 1976, Letraset Canada Limited all rights reserved

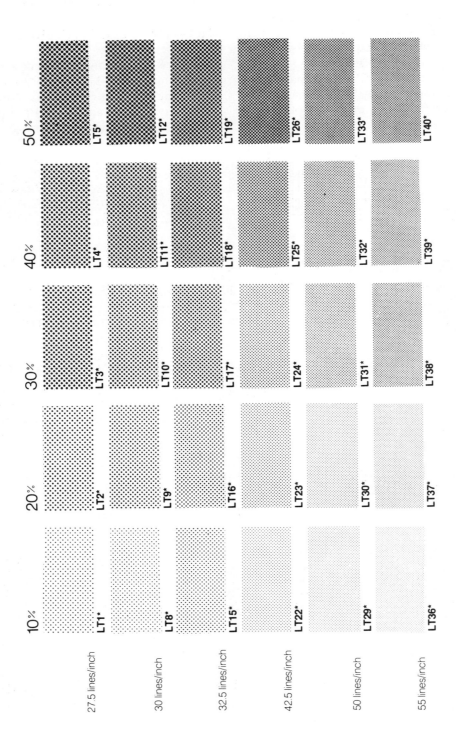

Figure 10.5 Screens used in plans and maps and available in dry transfer lettering.

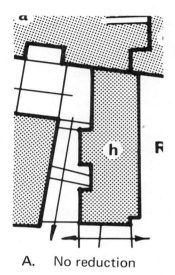

A.   No reduction

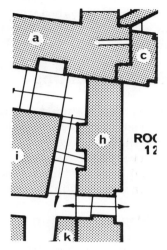

B.   75% of original

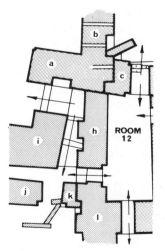

C.   50% of original

D.   25% of original

Figure 10.6 Screens selected for a drawing will depend on the amount of reduction for publication. The effect of different reductions on a screen (Letratone 16) is shown above. (Letraset, Instant Lettering, Letratone, Spacematic are the registered trade marks of Letraset Canada Limited.)

such as dot screens, patterns resembling brick walls, and patterns used on topographic maps.

To use the dry-transfer pattern simply cut a segment off the plastic sheet and apply it to the art work. Trace the outline of the area to be toned onto the transfer and then trim off the excess material with a sharp edge. As before, burnish the transfer and spray it with a fixative.

Maps and Map-Making

An archaeological report should provide a location map and a site map to enable the reader to focus in on the site and its geographical setting. These maps can be produced with the aid of base maps and aerial photographs, the sources of which have been discussed in chapters 2 and 3.

The Location Map

The first map to appear in a report should show the site's general geographical location. This can be done by a composite of three small maps in the following order: a general map showing the site in relation to the province as a whole; a map of the county or township showing the location of the site and its relationship to the larger towns or settlements; and a large scale map showing the site in its immediate environs, including the relationship of the site to roads, hydro lines, settlements, and important physical features. Usually the first map of the series is the largest, followed in decreasing size by the second and third. Indicate the area reproduced on the second and third maps on the first and second map respectively. A composite map is shown in figure 10.7.

The Site Map

The location map should be followed by a site map to show the site and its archaeological features in relation to the immediate surroundings. Include such features as buildings and roads in and around the site, the site limits, areas outside the site where testing was done, trees, shrubs, fence lines, telephone and hydro poles, and any Geodetic Survey bench mark in the area. The exact geographical location, elevation and number of the bench mark should be shown. A site map was previously shown in figure 8.1.

DRAWING THE MAPS

Base maps provide the details necessary for the preparation of maps for the archaeological report; once you have suitable ones you can begin the preparation of location and site maps, keeping in mind certain general guidelines:

1. A north arrow is an essential item on every drawing. All maps should be drawn so that north is the top of the drawing, except in rare cases where this is impracticable or would waste space in a publication. In these cases the north can be toward the side. The north arrow should be in the same place, when possible, on all drawings in the same report.

2. The size and placement of lettering on maps should be consistent throughout. Include the name of the province in large letters. The name of the county can be smaller and placed under that of the province. If possible, all bodies of water should be labelled in italics, and all land features in roman letters. Label major cities in upper case characters and small towns in upper and lower case. Lettering should be clear and properly spaced so that when the map is reduced in size the information remains legible.

3. A scale (in metric units) should be present on all maps. It is not sufficient to express the scale as a ratio, e.g. 1:250 or 1:500, as the meaning of the ratio changes when the drawing is reduced or enlarged. If you want to use a ratio on a drawing then calculate the reduction and select a ratio for the drawing in its final form. For example, if a drawing is done at a scale of 1:250 and it is to be reduced 50 per cent when published, then its published scale is 1:500. This latter ratio is placed on the drawing, and appears in the published version, although the original art work remains at 1:250.

4. The thickness of lines on maps should vary according to the physical features being drawn. For example, when preparing location maps draw shore lines such as those along large lakes and coast lines with a technical pen using a No.

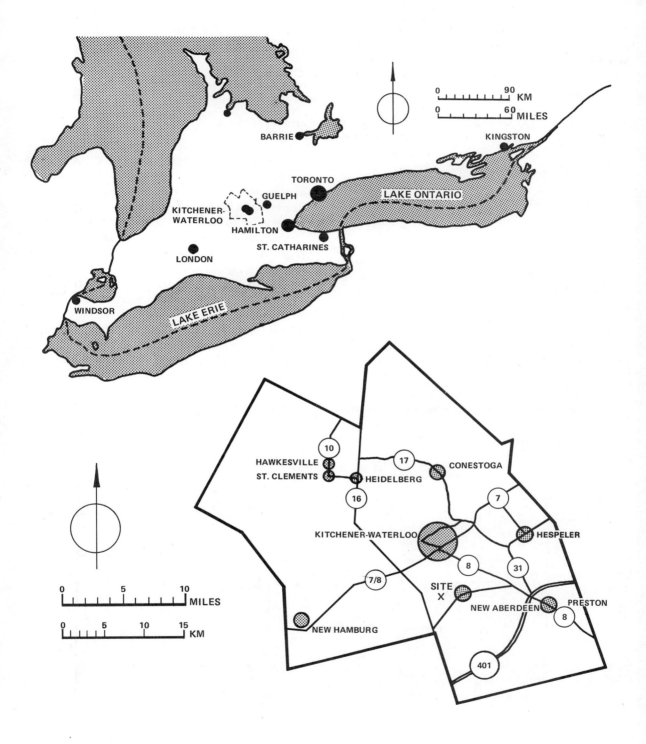

Figure 10.7 Composite location map.

3 nib. For major rivers use a No. 2 nib, and for major roads a No. 1 nib. Draw provincial boundaries as a dotted line, using a No. 2 nib, and international boundaries as a dashed line with a No. 3 nib. Small bends on natural features should be straightened or eliminated to simplify the map.

5. On the site map show the excavation grid and label the grid intervals. If an over-all grid is not used, then each area excavated should be clearly indicated and labelled.

6. Follow standardized map symbols as closely as possible in all maps prepared for publication.

7. All drawings should be drawn to the same scale or, if required, to one of several scales that are multiples of each other. For example, the scales 1:20, 1:100, 1:200 may be necessary to draw a baulk, trench, or site layout respectively.

Drawing Sections and Architectural Features

As a general rule, original drawings should be at least twice the final size required for publication. The width of all ink lines in drawings will have to be determined to allow for the reduction re-quired. As an example, for drawings that are to be reduced 50 per cent the following technical pen nib sizes are suggested:

outlines of walls	3
lines denoting change in elevation	1
surface details and cross-hatching	0
grid lines	2x0
grid coordinates	1

If a drawing is to be reduced more than 50 per cent then the thickness of lines on the original work will have to be greater than those listed above. The best procedure is to choose a standard reduction for all drawings of a report. This is referred to as the "common reduction" and enables the cameraman to photograph the drawings without changing the setting of his copy camera, a great time-saver.

These are the procedures for preparing drawings of features from field plans:

1. Field drawings have a lot of detail that may be unnecessary in published drawings; accordingly, the first task of the author of the report is to indicate to the illustrator which features should be included.

Attach the field drawing to the drawing board with masking tape (never pins) and cover it with drafting film, which should also be firmly at-

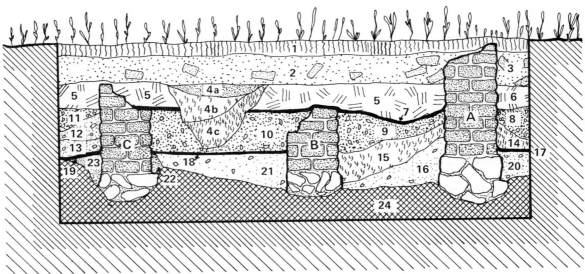

Figure 10.9a An archaeological section ready for publication.

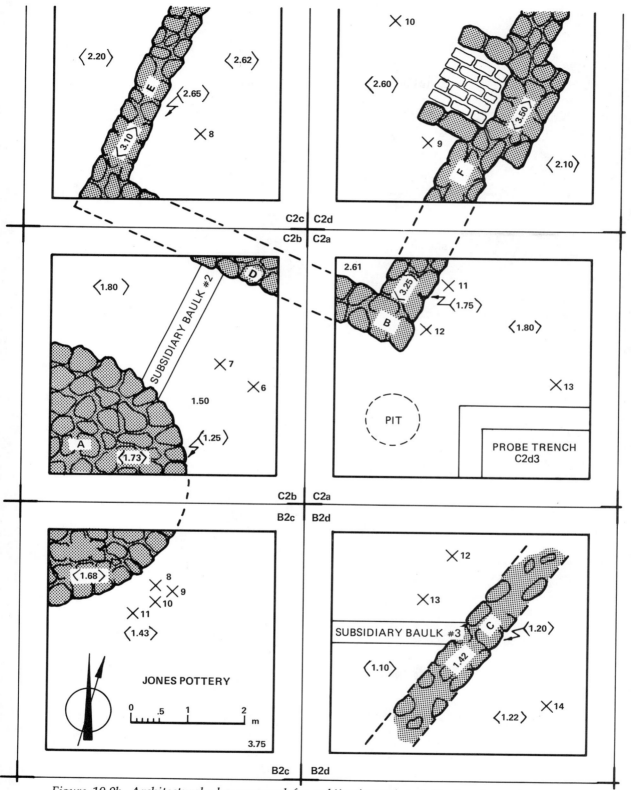

Figure 10.9b. Architectural plan prepared for publication using field plan shown in figure 8.1.

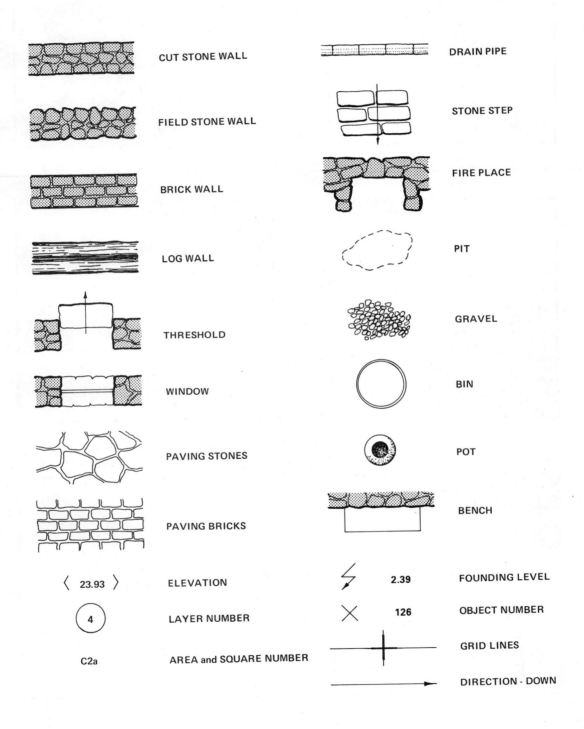

CUT STONE WALL

FIELD STONE WALL

BRICK WALL

LOG WALL

THRESHOLD

WINDOW

PAVING STONES

PAVING BRICKS

⟨ 23.93 ⟩   ELEVATION

④   LAYER NUMBER

C2a   AREA and SQUARE NUMBER

DRAIN PIPE

STONE STEP

FIRE PLACE

PIT

GRAVEL

BIN

POT

BENCH

2.39   FOUNDING LEVEL

126   OBJECT NUMBER

GRID LINES

DIRECTION - DOWN

Figure 10.8 Sample architectural convention symbols.

tached with tape. Be sure that both the original drawing and the film are flat on the board.

2. Begin the ink drawing by tracing the perimeter of the feature.

3. Trace the outline of the individual bricks or rocks to complete the drawing of walls. Bricks or rocks can be cross-hatched to make them stand out from other parts of the drawing. For cross-hatching use a nib no more than one-half the width of the one used for the outline of bricks and rocks.

4. Add other architectural details, varying the thickness of the ink line according to the importance given them in the final drawings.

5. Be sure to indicate the north and include a metric scale bar on each drawing.

6. Fine grid lines corresponding to the excavation grid should be superimposed on architectural plans. Where grid lines intersect accentuate them by using a thicker line (see figure 10.9b). Label the grid intervals along the edges of the drawing so as not to clutter the centre of the drawing.

7. Conventional symbols make it possible to give a clear interpretation of each part of the drawing. Fig. 10.8 shows a number of them suggested for architectural plans. These conventions remain clear and understandable when reduced to as little as 25 per cent of their original size.

Drawing Artifacts

Artifacts are drawn to reproduce their shape, decoration, and visual appearance. Even the best photograph may not show these details; it is the illustrator's skill that creates a clear presentation.

Pottery sherds and restored or complete pottery vessels are among the commonest artifacts from historical sites. The director of an excavation should tell the illustrator which sherds or complete pots need to be drawn.

GENERAL RULES FOR DRAWING POTTERY

Visualize a pot as divided into four equal parts, as shown in figure 10.10, with one-quarter removed so that when viewed from the front the section exposing the interior is on the left of the

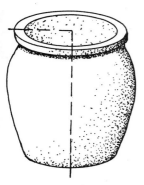

Cut 1/4 out of pot.

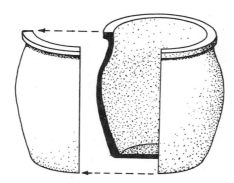

Remove, exposing left side of interior.

Pot as it should be drawn.

Figure 10.10 Hypothetical sectioning of a pot prior to drawing.

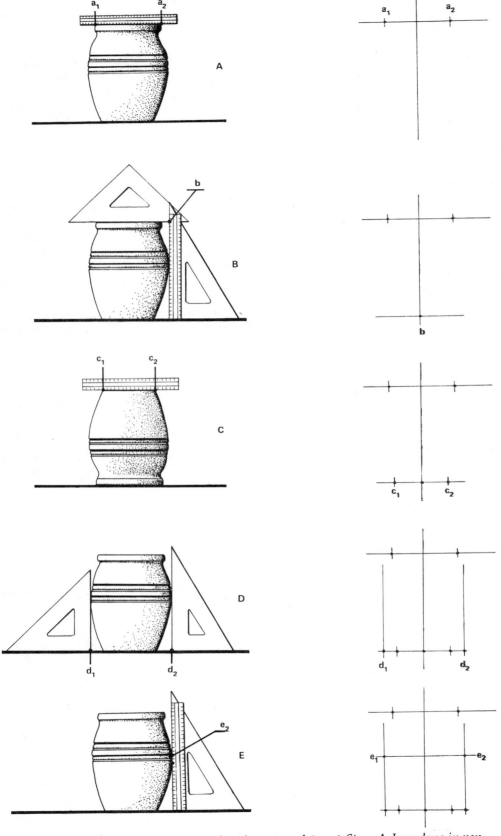

Figures 10.11 & 10.12 Instructions on drawing a complete pot. Steps A-I are done in pencil. The finished drawing (step J) is done in ink and all pencil construction lines are erased.

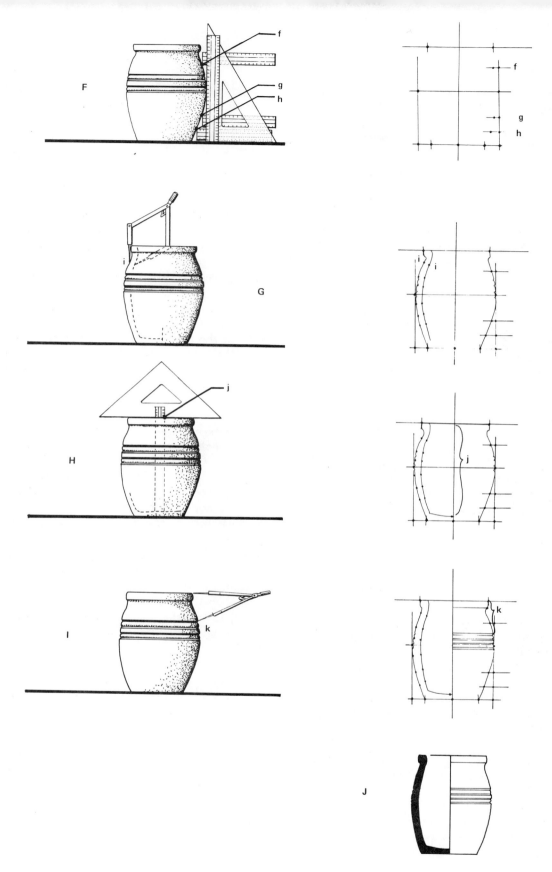

Figure 10.12.

centre line. The exterior is shown on the right of the centre line. In shading to give depth and texture assume that a light source is shining from the upper left-hand side of the paper at an angle of 45 degrees to the centre line of the pot.

The procedures for drawing a pot are illustrated in figure 10.11 and 10.12 and described below:

1. The first step in drawing a pot is to prepare a drawing using a 4H pencil with a fine point. Use only light pressure on the pencil, as these lines have to be removed later when the inking of the drawing has been completed.

2. Begin by drawing a horizontal line on a piece of drawing paper. Strathmore two-ply paper or 1000H Clear-print tracing paper are good for this purpose. The horizontal line should be at a point high enough to permit the full height of the vessel to be drawn under it. This line represents the rim line of the pot.

3. In the middle of the drawing surface place a set square against a T-square and draw a line perpendicular to the rim line and extending below it. This perpendicular line is the centre line for the drawing.

4. Measure the diameter of the rim of the pot with a ruler. On the rim line mark off one-half of the diameter of the rim (radius) on both sides of the centre line as shown in Figure 10.11A.

5. Measure the height of the vessel by placing a set square vertically against the upright pot. Place a ruler along the edge of the set square, and with a second set square placed across the rim, read the height of the pot where the rim set square intersects the ruler. If a ruler is not calibrated from its end, do not forget to compensate for any difference (figure 10.11B).

6. Measuring down from the rim line, mark the height of the pot along the centre line and draw a base line.

7. Measure the base diameter in the same manner as the rim, and mark it off on the base line (figure 10.11C).

8. Measure the maximum diameter of the pot by placing the pot upright on a piece of gridded tracing paper. Using the grid lines as a reference, place a set square vertically against the pot and put a pencil mark at the inside bottom edge of the set square (see figure 10.11D). Repeat this on the opposite side of the vessel. The distance between the two points thus obtained is the maximum diameter. Using a ruler placed in the same position as in step 10.11B, note the height of the vessel at which the maximum diameter occurs, and transfer all the measurements to the drawing (figure 10.11E).

9. Using the same position of scale and set square as in 13E, take a second scale and measure the body of the pot at a number of points to determine the profile of the pot (see figure 10.12). Be sure to take measurements along the edge of the ruler that is touching the vessel. Transfer these values to the drawing.

10. When one side of the vessel has been drawn the other side can be traced from the curve of the first side. (This can only be done if the sides of the vessel are similar). Take a second piece of tracing paper and mark it with a cross at the intersection of the rim line and the centre line, and the base line and the centre line. Place it over the first drawing and trace the curved edge of the vessel with a soft lead pencil. Turn the tracing paper over and line up the two reference marks so that the curve is a mirror image of the other side. Rub the tracing paper with the side of a pencil to transfer the graphite of the now upside-down tracing paper on to the pottery drawing. Remove the scrap tracing paper and redraw the line left by the soft lead pencil.

11. Draw the section of the vessel on the left side by measuring the thickness of the wall at different heights (figure 10.12G). This can be done with a set of calipers bent so they can go over the rim of the pot. Transfer these measurements to the drawing by laying the caliper points against the drawing at the correct height.

12. To measure the thickness of the base of the pot place a set square over the rim of the vessel and lower a ruler into the vessel to the top of the

base. The difference between total height of the vessel found in the measurements in figure 10.11B; this value is the thickness of the base (see figure 10.12H).

13. Use a set of calipers to measure the distance from the rim to part of the groove design (see figure 10.12I). Transfer these measurements to the drawing, being careful to measure on the drawing along the profile, *not* along the centre line. To copy any painted decoration found on a pot, place a piece of tracing paper on the pot and lightly trace the design. Rub the back of this tracing paper with a soft lead pencil to make a carboned surface. Transfer the design to the drawing by placing the drawing with the carboned side down and tracing over the design with a pencil. Remove the tracing paper and go over the line work with a sharp pencil.

Once completed, each pencil drawing should be checked a second time, preferably by another person, to evaluate the accuracy of the reproduction.

INKING THE POTTERY DRAWING

After completing the pencil outline start inking in the rim line with the aid of a T-square, but begin the line on the left side of the drawing approximately 1 centimetre from the inside edge of the section. Continue the rim line across the centre line to the furthest point of the right-hand side.

Use a set square to draw the vertical centre line with the same nib number as the rim line. Draw in the full extent of the base line, except in cases where the base is not flat or is actually a pedestal. In the latter case you should draw the base line as you do the rim line, leaving a 1-centimetre space on the inside of the section.

The curved lines of the pot should then be drawn in free-hand, using a No. 3 nib. On the left side of the drawing, outline the outside of the section beginning at the base and working up; conversely, draw the inside of the section from the rim downward. The space between these lines can now be inked with a small paint brush or a thick nib. If possible, the right side of the pot should be drawn as one continuous, smooth line, but to do this requires considerable practice. When the pot outline has been inked

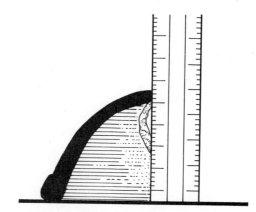

Figure 10.13 Measuring the height of a sherd

the surface decoration can be inked using a No. 1 nib. Finally, remove the pencil lines with a soft, non-smearing eraser for the finished drawing (see fig. 10.12J).

DRAWING SHERDS

When the evidence for a particular vessel consists only of fragments, it is necessary to reconstruct the probable appearance of the complete vessel from these sherds. A rim sherd, for instance, can be used to find the original shape and angle of the top of a vessel, whereas a base sherd will provide the angle of the body of the wall just above the base, and the thickness of the base itself. The curvature of a complete rim-to-base sherd can be used to establish the diameter of the complete vessel.

Rim Sherd

A rim sherd can be drawn by the following procedure:

1. Determine the stance, that is, the original position of the sherd as part of an entire vessel, by placing it, rim down, on a table top (plate 10.7). Place a light source behind the sherd and tilt the sherd until you find a position where no light is able to pass between the sherd and the table. The angle of the sherd from the table is the stance of the rim.

2. Draw a rim line and a centre line following the same procedures as for a complete pot.

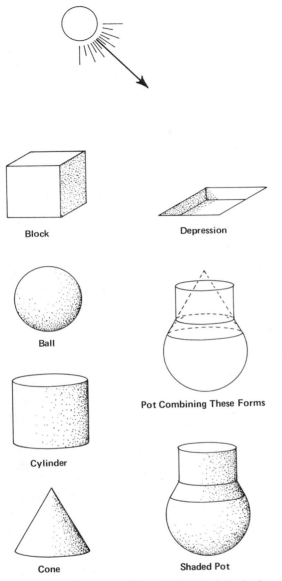

Block

Depression

Ball

Pot Combining These Forms

Cylinder

Cone

Shaded Pot

Figure 10.14 The effect of light and shadow on geometric shapes. Most objects will be a composite of one or several of these shapes.

3. Place a rim sherd on a diameter chart, holding the sherd in its correct stance, and determine the diameter of the sherd and therefore the diameter of the original vessel. (A diameter chart can be made by starting with a centre point and drawing concentric circles, each with a diameter 2 centimetres greater than the previous one, until

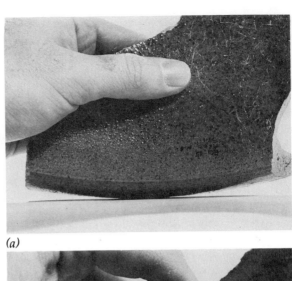

(a)

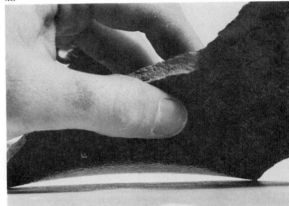

(b)

(c)

Plate 10.7 Determining the stance of a sherd of a pot. (a) Incorrect stance as the sherd is leaning back too far and light shows at the edges; (b) incorrect stance, as sherd is leaning forward too far and light shows in the centre; (c) correct stance with no light showing between sherd and table.

the outermost circle is about 50 centimetres in diameter.) The diameter of the vessel should be determined from the curvature of the outside of the rim. Transfer the measurement to the drawing.

4. Measure the height of the sherd and its diameter at its maximum height. (This has been described in the instructions on drawing a complete pot.) Transfer these values to the drawing. Remember that you are measuring the sherd upside down and that all measurements will have to be reversed bottom to top on the drawing.

5. Use the Formagage or the method described under drawing a complete pot to determine the profile of the sherd.

6. For the rest of the drawing follow the procedures outlined for drawing a complete pot.

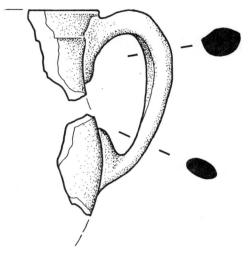

Figure 10.15 Sections through the object should be placed next to the largest view of the object, and thin lines used to indicate where the section was taken.

Base Sherd

Sherds from the base of a vessel are measured in the same way as the rim, except the drawing begins from the base line upward, whereas the rim sherd is drawn from the rim line downward.

DRAWING SMALL ARTIFACTS

Good drawings of small artifacts can be made with patience and a little practice. Study the artifact before starting, looking carefully at the design, shape, and surface texture. You will then want to decide what views are necessary to illustrate the object completely. Because the light source is assumed to be from the upper left corner of the drawing paper, the right side of all artifacts will be in shadow, and shadow will fill the left edge of depressions. Likewise, raised designs will cast a shadow to the right of the raised portion (see figure 10.14).

The following description of the steps in drawing a military button is used to show the procedures for drawing a typical small artifact (figure 10.16).

1. The button should be drawn twice its size so that when the drawing is reduced to 25 per cent (the common reduction) the object will be illustrated at one-half its original size. Measure the diameter of the button with a set of calipers and double this measurement.

2. If the button has a relief that can be rubbed, make a rubbing of the surface on a piece of gridded paper. Use the grid as a guide, and double the dimensions of the elements of the design when copying the design onto the drawing. If the relief cannot be rubbed, the design will have to be copied by free-hand drawing, using calipers to establish the size and location of all elements of the design.

3. Cross-check the accuracy of the pencil drawing against the size of actual design with a set of calipers.

4. When inking the drawing use a No. 1 technical pen nib for the outline and a 2x0 for the elements of the design. Make the lines on the shadow side of the drawing a little thicker than others. Apply stippling on areas that would be in deep shadow.

5. Clean the finished drawing by erasing any pencil lines with a soft gum eraser.

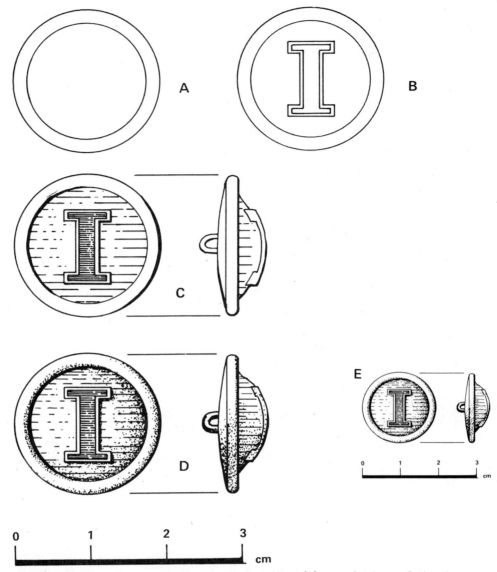

Figure 10.16 Drawing a button: (A) drawing the outline, (B) transferring a design in pencil, (C) drawing the side view in pencil, (D) the finished drawing in ink, (E) drawing reduced 50% to its original size for publication.

THE BODY OF THE REPORT

There are certain basic guidelines to follow when preparing the typescript of a report. It should be free of jargon and spelling, punctuation, footnoting and bibliographic references should follow the form stipulated by the journal or publisher to which the report is to be submitted. The manuscript should be typed on one side of 8½x11 smooth white bond, and double-spaced throughout, including footnotes and quotations. Most editors prefer these on separate sheets rather than added to the text pages. Publishers usually require that you submit one or more copies of a report in addition to the original. Each sheet of typescript should have a 1¼ to 1½-inch margin at the top, bottom and sides, with the author's name and the page number on the upper right-hand side. This allows different sections of the text to be sent to different readers who will comment on the contents, and makes it easy to re-assemble the separate parts.

Unless the specific nature of the dig results

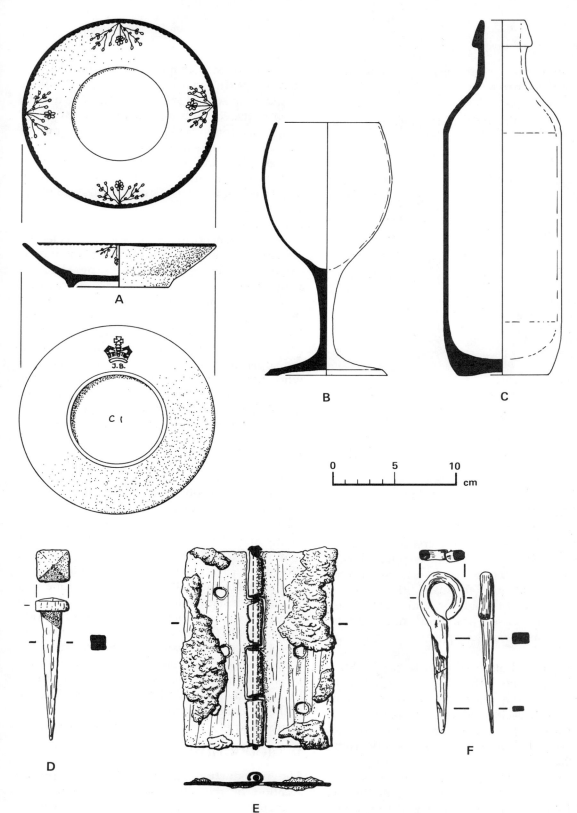

Figure 10.17 A complete figure of objects from an historic site. The figure is ready for publication.

dictates otherwise, a complete report should consist of three parts.

Preliminaries

Title page
Copyright Notice
Contents
Illustrations
   Figures
   Tables
   Plates
Preface

Text

Introduction
History of the Site
Methods of Excavation
Excavation Results
Interpretation
Discussion
Conclusions

End Pages

Appendix
Glossary
Bibliography
Index

Preliminaries

The preliminaries serve as a reference to the contents of the report, and should be included with the text when the report is sent to an editor. The title page should show the exact title of the report, and name of the author, and the name of the publishing house. The author's name should be written as it is to appear on the final published work.

All original scholarly works are copyrighted in the name of the author unless arrangements are made to the contrary. You and your publisher will decide the question jointly. In a published work the law requires that the owner of the copyright be shown on the copyright page, which is the next one after the title page. Details on registering a copyright under the *Copyright Act* may be obtained from the Bureau of Intellectual Property, Ministry of Consumer and Corporate Affairs, Ottawa.

The next page is the contents page. This page should list the title and page numbers of the beginning of each chapter as they appear in the manuscript. In lengthy reports where chapters may contain several sub-headings, these may be listed in the contents as a further guide.

After the contents page, the list of illustrations provides a convenient reference to all the figures, tables and plates in the report. If the report includes a large number of illustrations, it may be advisable to list figures, tables and plates on individual sheets.

The last part of the preliminaries is the preface, which normally consists of a brief explanation of the reasons for undertaking the excavation, the objectives of the dig, an acknowledgement of the persons and organizations sponsoring the dig, acknowledgement of financial assistance and the loan of equipment. Further, the preface should include a list of dig staff, provided this is not too long, or else a list of the supervisory staff, and a list of the persons who have helped make the dig possible, especially the landowner and tenants. Finally, the preface should contain a statement indicating the deposition of field notes and artifacts.

Text

The text should contain all information relevant to excavation. It should be divided into chapters, the contents of which will depend on the nature of the site, the results to be reported, and the manner in which the evidence is to be presented. No two excavation reports are identical as no two archaeological sites are the same. One way to obtain insight into the techniques of report writing is to read other published reports and to evaluate both the effectiveness of the format and the clarity and relevance of the contents. Each chapter should combine a clear and accurate presentation of the evidence pertaining to its theme with an interpretation of the significance of this evidence. A number of suggested chapters for the text of a report are discussed below.

INTRODUCTION

The introduction should include the precise location of the site, using the military grid reference, and the name of the province, county and township. The location can be described in a short written paragraph and a composite location map. A map of the same period as the site might also be of value, especially if it showed early trade relationships etc. Include a description of the typography and geology, especially where this is relevant to the history of the site, to give the reader a visual notion of the surface of the ground.

The introduction should also include a description of the circumstances that led to the excavations, a detailed report on all groups and individuals sponsoring the excavation, a description of the scale and objectives of the work attempted and a statement on the actual work accomplished. Finally, a statement on the efforts made to preserve or restore the site should be included. Brief mention of special subjects or areas dealt with in the text and possible areas of further inquiry should also be made.

HISTORY OF THE SITE

A balanced assessment of the documentary history of the site should follow immediately after the introduction. The historical information included, however, should have a direct bearing on the objectives of the excavations. Be cautious here; there are many historical details on a site and its owners that are interesting but of little relevance to the actual objectives of a dig. If such details are important as genealogy or folk history, they could be assembled and published in a different format.

METHODS OF EXCAVATION

A detailed presentation of the methods used in the excavations, the labelling system for the site, and the specialized techniques used to retrieve artifacts, objects or samples helps the reader understand your data. This presentation can discuss the limitations of the methods employed, and other external factors that have affected the excavation and consequently the information presented in the report. Shortcomings in technique, although a topic that most excavators prefer to omit, should be outlined frankly and straightforwardly; this will indicate the scope and range of the data in the report, and help others improve field techniques on their own digs.

EXCAVATION RESULTS

There is no ready-made guide to presenting excavation results, as the manner of presentation depends on the type actually obtained in the field. Statistical data is best put in tables or charts. Photographs and drawings keyed to the text will help to reduce the amount of written material and to make it more vivid. Here again the study of published historical site reports will suggest effective presentations.

The text of the excavation results should include the details of structures (with accompanying plan drawings), details of stratigraphy (with accompanying section drawings), and a description and provenance of all artifacts together with drawings and photographs of them. With industrial sites you might also report on the techniques employed by the industry, and present any evidence of technological development.

The order in which the results are presented may vary with the type of information obtained and the number of squares uncovered. Results of architectural features and stratigraphy could be reported one square at a time, or better, on a chronological basis, combining the results from a number of associated squares and describing the earliest period first. The artifacts contained in the site should be described in chronological and stratigraphic order to present the evidence for dating the associated architectural features. Photographs and drawings of architecture and artifacts are essential evidence of the actual relationships between layers and features, and should be included where they will be most useful.

INTERPRETATION AND DISCUSSION

The interpretive chapter of a report sums up the information from the entire dig to present a total picture of the site at each period in its history. This discussion should compare the data from the site with what is already known from other sites in the same locality or cultural area, or from similar types of sites in the same historical period. This evaluation will also consider what may be known from previous excavations at the site, the importance of the information gained from the present excavations, and a comparison of this information with that published in historical archaeological literature. For example, a report of the excavation of a pottery site may also include a specific discussion of the kiln construction at the site compared to what is known about kiln construction techniques at other potteries in North America.

CONCLUSIONS

This part of the report provides for a concise summary of what has been learned from the excavations. Just as the introduction had set out the objectives of the dig, and the discussion of excavation methods explained the techniques applied to reach these objectives, so the conclusion indicates the degree of success. It is the logical end of a well balanced and complete report. The conclusion can also include an assessment of the problems raised or left unsolved by the dig, and suggest the direction of further work.

End Pages

The end pages provide the reference material that allows more complete use of the report. This material may include specialists' reports, detailed notes, a bibliography of materials consulted in writing the report, and a glossary of key words and ideas.

APPENDIX

As an excavator is not usually a specialist in all the fields of study associated with historical archaeology, he must rely on the analysis of the artifacts conducted by specialists in related disciplines. The significant conclusions of these specialists' reports should be incorporated into the text of the report, while the actual details of the studies should go into the appendix, as they may be of interest primarily to other specialists. To include the full specialists' reports in the text would break the continuity of presentation and distract the reader from the main topic. Long notes should be placed in the appendix rather than in extended footnotes.

GLOSSARY

A glossary provides a ready reference to the terminology used in the report, saving the reader's time and avoiding confusion. It is especially helpful when a report is prepared for a non-professional audience, or when archaeological terms are used in a way not ordinarily understood by other archaeologists. Words such as "phase", "strata", "layer", "artifact", and "area" may be used to describe different things at different sites.

INDEX

Few archaeological reports have an index, and should one appear it is usually very badly prepared. The index helps the reader understand the variety and nature of the information in the report, and to select and locate a specific topic rather than reading the entire text to find what might be only a few sentences on the subject.

Preparing an index is usually the author's task; if you have no previous experience at indexing you might examine a number of them in archaeological books. This should suggest the most useful form for your purposes. Instructions on preparing an index are found in most style manuals or can be obtained from a number of books on indexing available through commercial book stores.

The writing of a dig report is often viewed with great apprehension. The task requires a thorough understanding of the nature of the evidence from the dig, a knowledge of published literature in historical archaeology, and painstaking attention to details of good writing and grammar. Few reports are published without some re-writing; it is the attention you give to the whole process that will determine the ultimate usefulness of your information. In future years, people will evaluate both the excavation itself and the skill of those responsible for the dig primarily on the basis of the published report.

Chapter 11

RESOURCES FOR INVOLVEMENT

A great number of Canadian organizations deal with historical archaeology in some form. The interest of various archaeological societies, museums and universities in archaeology indicates their commitment to retrieving some of the rapidly disappearing evidence of the past.

A distinct discipline of "historical" as opposed to "prehistoric" archaeology has not yet evolved in Canada, and historical archaeology is often found under the broader discipline of anthropology. Only in the past few years has there been an indication that historical archaeology is coming to be recognized as a subject with problems, methodology, and subject matter distinct from those of other forms of North American archaeology. It is not difficult, therefore, to understand why so few references to historical archaeology activities in Canada can be made at this time without at the same time referring to anthropology.

ARCHAEOLOGICAL SOCIETIES

Local and provincial archaeology societies can help provide resources for field surveys and rescue excavations, where volunteers are required at short notice. Volunteers can make significant contributions by keeping watch against thoughtless or unknowing destruction of archaeological resources in their own areas.

The local, provincial or national archaeological society is the basic organizational unit in which professional and non-professional archaeologists can work together. The provincial societies, of which there are five, may also have local chapters which sponsor seminars, lectures,

Plate 11.1. Excavation underway at Fort York

excavations, and often issue newsletters or bulletins that transmit the work of the archaeologist to the wider community. The Ontario Archaeological Society publishes a newsletter, and a journal, *Ontario Archaeology*, that is of professional standard and contains scholarly articles on a wide variety of topics. These generally deal with prehistoric archaeology, although articles on historical archaeology are welcomed and may be published in either the newsletter or journal.

The Canadian Archaeological Association, with headquarters in Ottawa, is the national organization of archaeologists. This Association produces an annual bulletin dealing with areas of current research, and sponsors an annual conference at which everyone interested in archaeology, professional or non-professional alike, is invited to participate in seminars. A growing number of papers published by the Association are on subjects related to historical archaeology.

If you are interested in historical archaeology activities contact the nearest provincial archaeological society, or the Canadian Archaeological Association, for information on how to become involved. Canadian archaeological societies are:

National

Canadian Archaeological Association
National Museum of Man
Ottawa
Ontario

Provincial

Archaeological Society of Alberta
Edmonton Centre
11526 77th Avenue
Edmonton
Alberta

Archaeological Society of British Columbia
504 2005 Pendrell Street
Vancouver
British Columbia

Manitoba Archaeological Society
190 Rupert Avenue
Winnipeg
Manitoba

Ontario Archaeological Society
P.O. Box 241
Postal Station "P"
Toronto
Ontario

Saskatchewan Archaeological Society
857 Elphinstone Street
Regina

MUSEUMS

The local museum or historical society can be a catalyst for archaeological activities in the community. Providing contacts among local people interested in history, and possibly historical archaeology, the museum should be a meeting place for those interested in organizing field surveys or excavations. Space for study and storage of artifacts, and advice on conservation and restoration of important objects may be available

there. The historical archaeologist may also get practical assistance in locating historical documents or objects. After the archaeological society the local museum is the next contact for anyone interested in pursuing further study in historical archaeology. The curator can help uncover opportunities for work in historical archaeology, if only by providing a list of organizations known to be active in survey work or excavation.

There are too many local museums to list in this book, but the address of the nearest museum can be obtained from the local public library or by consulting *Canadian Museums and Related Institutions*, published by the Canadian Museums Association, Ottawa, or the *Directory of Museums, Art Galleries and Related Institutions*, published by Statistics Canada, Ottawa.

National and provincial museums sponsor a wide range of archaeological activities, some of them concerned with Canadian historical archaeology. These museums are able to supply information on historical archaeological activities in their respective constituencies. As well as important collections that can be consulted for study, they have reference libraries, archives, and trained curatorial staff familiar with the range of materials found at historic sites in Canada.

Conditions of access to artifact collections or libraries vary with the particular institution. Anyone interested in using these facilities should write to the museum before making a visit. The national and provincial museums are:

National

Victoria Memorial Museum Building
National Museum of Man
McLeod and Metcalfe
Ottawa
Ontario

National Museum of Science and Technology
1867 St. Laurent Blvd.
Ottawa
Ontario

National Postal Museum
Sir Alexander Campbell Building
Confederation Heights
Ottawa
Ontario

Provincial

Provincial Museum of Alberta
12845 102 Avenue
Edmonton
Alberta

British Columbia Provincial Museum
Heritage Court
601 Belleville Street
Victoria
British Columbia

Manitoba Museum of Man and Nature
190 Rupert Avenue
Winnipeg
Manitoba

New Brunswick Museum
277 Douglas Avenue
St. John
New Brunswick

Newfoundland Museum
Duckworth Street
St. John's
Newfoundland

Nova Scotia Museum
1747 Summer Street
Halifax
Nova Scotia

Royal Ontario Museum
100 Queen's Park Crescent
Toronto
Ontario

Confederation Art Gallery and Museum
P.O. Box 848
Charlottetown
Prince Edward Island

Musée de Québec
Parc des Champs de Bataille
Québec
Québec

Saskatchewan Museum of Natural History
Wascana Park
Regina
Saskatchewan

Museum of the North
Yellowknife
Northwest Territories

FURTHER TRAINING IN ARCHAEOLOGY

A large number of universities in Canada have departments of anthropology providing both academic instruction and field projects in subjects of interest to the historical archaeologist. In Ontario, Wilfrid Laurier University, Waterloo, has an undergraduate course in historical archaeology which combines classroom instruction in field and laboratory techniques with a period of on-site excavation at a local historic site. In addition to academic instruction in archaeology, universities and community colleges offer opportunities for participation in public lectures, field trips and seminars on topics pertaining to historical archaeology.

Historical archaeology is taught in most Canadian universities, although it might be included in a general archaeology course. If you are interested in a career in historical archaeology, contact the anthropology department of your chosen university and ask for details on the programme of study in subjects related to historical archaeology, admission requirements, and the opportunities for field excavation experience during the course. If you are in high school now, get a good background in Canadian history, geography, and the physical sciences. Don't overlook the opportunities for instruction in architectural drafting, surveying, and photography available at community colleges and other institutions of continuing education.

These are the Canadian universities with a department of anthropology or combined anthropology and sociology departments:

Alberta

University of Alberta, Edmonton, Alta.
University of Calgary, Calgary, Alta.
University of Lethbridge, Lethbridge, Alta.

British Columbia

University of British Columbia, Vancouver, B.C.
Simon Fraser University, Burnaby, B.C.
University of Victoria, Victoria, B.C.

Manitoba

University of Manitoba, Winnipeg, Manitoba
University of Winnipeg, Winnipeg, Manitoba

New Brunswick

University of New Brunswick, Fredericton, N.B.

Newfoundland

Memorial University of Newfoundland, St. John's, Nfld.

Nova Scotia

Dalhousie University, Halifax, N.S.
Mount Saint Vincent University, Halifax, N.S.
St. Francis Xavier University, Antigonish, N.S.

Ontario

Carlton University, Ottawa, Ont.
University of Guelph, Guelph, Ont.
Lakehead University, Thunder Bay, Ont.
Université Laurentienne, Sudbury, Ont.
McMaster University, Hamilton, Ont.
Wilfrid Laurier University, Waterloo, Ont.
University of Toronto, Toronto, Ont.
Trent University, Peterborough, Ont.
University of Waterloo, Waterloo, Ont.
University of Western Ontario, London, Ont.
University of Windsor, Windsor, Ont.
York University, Downsview, Ont.

Prince Edward Island

University of Prince Edward Island, Charlottetown, P.E.I.

Quebec

Université Laval, Québec, P.Q.
McGill University, Montreal, P.Q.
Université de Montréal, Montreal, P.Q.
Sir George Williams University, Montreal, P.Q.

Saskatchewan

University of Saskatchewan, Regina Campus, Regina, Sask.
University of Saskatchewan, Saskatoon Campus, Saskatoon, Sask.

Practical Experience

To develop good field techniques you must get practical experience, in handling archaeological materials and in excavation. Contact a local or provincial museum where there may be opportunities for volunteer work. Such a museum may encourage and guide volunteers willing to devote time each week to assisting in the restoration and interpretation of archaeological finds. Volunteers who work throughout the year on a wide variety of materials can, with experience, assume more responsibilities in field work and in the operation of the lab.

Museums, universities and archaeological societies sponsor summer excavations at historical sites. The actual nature of the excavations and the number of volunteers required vary from site to site; inquire early each year about dig opportunities. The number of excavations being conducted in Canada at any one time is small compared to the number of volunteers who would like to participate.

Some universities, such as Wilfrid Laurier in Waterloo, Ontario, the University of Winnipeg, Winnipeg, and the University of New Brunswick, Fredericton, sponsor field schools and training digs which provide an opportunity for on-site instruction and university course credit.

In Canada, there is no central registry of all archaeological digs that would welcome volunteer help, although such a registry would aid dig sponsors and volunteers alike. If you want to volunteer for one of the medieval or post-medieval sites in Britain, the Council for British Archaeology, 7 Marylebone Rd, London NW1 5HY England, publishes a *Calendar of Excavations* listing digs, conferences and study courses in archaeology. The Calendar is sent by air mail or surface post upon payment of a small subscription fee.

Training in subjects related to historical archaeology and of interest to museum personnel, is offered by provincial museums associations in Canada. These organizations provide seminars of varying length on a variety of subjects related to museums and museum work. A list of seminar topics may be obtained by writing to the nearest provincial museum association listed here:

National

Canadian Museums Association
56 Sparks Street
Ottawa
Ontario

Provincial

Alberta Museums Association
4804 49th Street
Camrose
Alberta

British Columbia Museums Association
B.C. Provincial Museum
Victoria
B.C.

Association of Manitoba Museums
c/o Crossley's Museum
R.R. #4
Grandview
Manitoba

Association of Museums of New Brunswick
c/o New Brunswick Provincial Museum
277 Douglas Avenue
St. John
N.B.

Ontario Museums Association
14A Hazelton Avenue
Toronto
Ontario

Société des Musées du Québec
Box 1153
Station B
Montreal
P.Q.

Saskatchewan Museums Association
c/o R.C.M.P. Museum
Regina
Saskatchewan

Canada offers many opportunities for historical archaeology work and study. If you have the enthusiasm and determination the work demands, you will find historical archaeology a stimulating, satisfying, and exciting part of life.

Glossary

archaeology The study of the people of the past through the recovery and analysis of the artifacts they left behind.

architectural feature Any structure associated with a site, including walls, wells, post holes, pits, etc.

area The basic unit of the grid contained within four surveyed grid stakes. Each area is further divided into four *squares* (q.v.).

artifact (also *find*) Anything made by man for his own use. In historical archaeology the word artifact is applied to materials such as glass, bone, pottery, metals, wood, stone, etc. that have been worked by man. See also *object*.

auger (*soil auger*) A tool with a thread or drill chamber on one end of a steel rod and a handle at the other end. Used to obtain a sample of material beneath the ground without extensive excavation.

baulk A unit of earth left standing between squares so that the evidence and sequence of various layers can be studied and recorded by the archaeologist.

bench mark A reference point permanently set in the ground, or established on a structure, that gives the location and elevation above sea level.

biscuit A term applied to pottery that has been fired but not glazed or otherwise finished.

body sherd A sherd from the side (or body) of a vessel. See also *sherd* and *diagnostic sherd*.

bonding A term used to describe the pattern of bricks or stones in a wall; also the manner in which two walls are joined together by stones or bricks which overlap or are common to both walls.

ceramics A term used by archaeologists for objects, especially pottery, made from clay.

contours Points of equal elevation on the ground. These points can be connected on a map to form a contour map.

contour survey A survey of a site at measured intervals to determine the changes in elevation.

course A horizontal layer of bricks or stones in a structure at the same elevation.

culture To the archaeologist, the activities of people as shown through the artifacts they leave behind.

datum A fixed point from which all levels are measured. A datum line is a line of fixed elevation secured by nails in the baulk of a square to help in making a scaled drawing of the baulk face.

diagnostic sherd A sherd from any part of the body of a vessel that is useful in determining the identity, dimensions, and decorative features of a vessel. The usual diagnostic sherds are the rim, base, neck, handle, spout, and lid, and body sherds with distinctive decoration.

dumpy level An instrument used to determine the difference in elevation between two positions in a site, or between a position in a site and a bench mark.

elevation This term has two meanings in this text: (1) The height in metres above a fixed point; (2) A scaled drawing of an architectural feature or structure as viewed in the vertical plane.

excavation The removal of soil and debris layers in such a way that artifacts and the relationship of layers to each other and to architectural features are observed and recorded.

feature See *architectural feature*.

field survey The study of archaeological remains on a site by observing the evidence visible without excavation.

fill Soil or debris placed in a trench, pit, or other depression, to create a level surface in preparation for further use.

foundation trench (builder's trench) A trench dug for the footing of a wall or other structure. After the wall or structure is built the trench is filled to the level of the surrounding ground.

founding level The elevation of the lowermost point of a structure.

geophysics The study of the physical properties of the earth. As applied to historical archaeology, geophysical techniques are those used for exploration prior to excavation. Two common instruments used for geophysical prospecting in Canada are the magnetometer and the resistivity meter.

glaze A glassy surface given to ceramic objects, generally pottery, to make them waterproof. The glaze is applied as a liquid and when dry heated in a kiln to a temperature high enough to fuse it into a smooth glassy surface.

green A term applied to pottery that has been air-dried but not fired.

grid A series of regular areas, marked on the ground by strings, that have been carefully surveyed or measured by hand in preparation for excavation.

hachures A map-maker's symbol used to show the changes in elevation, in this book to illustrate man-made features.

kiln A temporary or permanent structure composed of a central chamber, fire-mouth (fire-box), and a chimney. The kiln is used to produce a high temperature to bake, and sometimes glaze, pottery or bricks.

layer A deposit of soil or debris with distinctive characteristics that set it apart from layers above or below it. These distinctive characteristics include colour, texture and artifacts.

level This term is used in this text to describe any horizontal plane. Compare this use of the word with the term *layer*, the latter being used exclusively to describe individual deposits of soil or debris.

line of collimation The line through the axis of the telescope and through the horizontal hair line of the level.

magnetometer An instrument for measuring the intensity of the earth's magnetic field at any particular point.

object An artifact which, because of its importance, condition, size, or other special characteristic, is handled separately during the course of the excavation. The nature of the site being dug determines the distinction to be made between objects and the remaining artifacts.

period A particular historical time-span represented by artifacts and associated architectural features. A period is composed of one or more *phases* (q.v.).

phase An observable combination of layers of soil or debris in a section which represent a definite historical entity within a period. There is an *archaeological phase* where one or more layers are associated with the construction, use, modification, or destruction of an architectural feature, and *a phase of abandonment*, representing one or more layers prior to the use of or after the abandonment of a particular architectural feature.

pit An irregularly-shaped cut into the ground for fill or other refuse; see also *test pit* and *post hole*.

plan A scaled drawing of a structure or other feature as viewed in the horizontal plane (i.e. from above).

post hole A special type of pit which at one time held an upright wooden post. The post hole can be recognized by the different colour and texture of its contents — the result of the decaying wood left in the hole — and the contrast to the surrounding layer into which the post hole was cut.

pottery Vessels formed of clay which are allowed to harden and then fired in a kiln.

probe bar A tool consisting of a pointed steel bar and a handle, used to detect an underground feature without excavation.

probe trench A form of test pit (q.v.) used to identify the vertical layering in a small part of a square before extensive excavation in the horizontal direction.

pug mill A large tub or barrel with a perpendicular shaft mounted with blades. The shaft when turned by horse power compresses, slices, and mixes plastic clays to a uniform consistency.

resistivity surveying The study of the pattern of electrical resistance beneath the surface of the ground in order to detect features of possible archaeological significance.

romer A device used for measuring the position of a point on a map within a one-kilometre square by dividing the square into tenths.

row   A term used to describe the width of a structure, such as a wall, in terms of the number of bricks or stones placed side by side in the same horizontal plane.

saggar   A container, usually made of fireclay, used for holding smaller pottery wares when stacking them in a kiln. A saggar prevents the pottery from sticking together during the fusing of the glaze and protects it from direct heat and flames.

sealed   A layer or part of a structure protected against contamination by material from subsequent layers is said to be sealed. A floor forms a typical barrier sealing the layer beneath it.

section   (archaeological section) The vertical face of a baulk showing layers and architectural features and their relationships; also, a scaled drawing made to record the appearance of the baulks.

sherd   (*shard*) A fragment of pottery.

site   Any land previously used by man that is of interest to archaeologists, or that has been located by field survey or excavation.

square   The smallest unit of the *grid*. Four equal size squares make up a grid *area*.

stilt   A triangular-shaped clay support for separating pottery during firing to keep the glaze from being damaged.

stratification   The deposition of soil and debris in successive layers. In an undisturbed condition the oldest layer is successively covered by more recent ones.

stratum   (plural: *strata*) See *layer*.

test pit   A small unit, often square in shape, excavated from the corner of a series of squares to establish the limits of occupation at a site.

transit   A surveyor's instrument used to measure horizontal and vertical angles and horizontal distances. The transit can be used as a level. It has a compass built into it so that one can measure angles related to magnetic north.

trench   A long and narrow excavation through a site, often along one of the major axes; used as a method of excavation when only a limited amount of time is available to explore a site.

typology   The classification of artifacts into groups on the basis of characteristics such as shape, colour, or other physical measurements.

wedge   A hand-formed clay fragment, usually in the shape of a wedge, (hence the name), used for separating pottery wares during firing.

APPENDIX

Federal and Provincial Legislation Affecting Archaeological Activities

Laws governing archaeological activities have been enacted by all provinces of Canada, and a number of federal laws applying to land under federal jurisdiction can be used to stop unauthorized excavation. Excavation of any land governed by the provincial laws can be carried out only after a permit or license for the work has been obtained. In some cases it is necessary to obtain a permit to conduct field and site surveys. The conditions and requirements which must be met before a permit will be issued vary, but most laws require the submission of a statement of the methods to be employed during the excavation, the disposition of objects and artifacts, and the submission of a report on the excavation results. The complete and up-to-date provincial regulations should be consulted before a permit application is submitted, and several months should be allowed for circulation and study of the application before approval can be expected.

In addition to the specific laws and regulations governing archaeology, there are laws regulating trespassing and protection of property rights. As these laws could be applied to stop any unauthorized or undesirable excavation, it is important to contact the provincial government department concerned in order to obtain all regulations affecting digging. Also, contact with government organizations can provide a channel of communication between specific projects and the larger sphere of archaeological activity within the province. Cooperation between excavators and government should result in the sharing of resources and experience, an important form of communication in any field of study.

Special mention should be made of the excavation of human burials. As excavation of human skeletal remains frequently comes under separate legislation, legal advice should be sought before a dig begins if there is a possibility of uncovering burial sites.

Legislation governing archaeological activities in federal and provincial jurisdictions is described below.

Federal Laws

There are no federal laws specifically governing archaeological activities in Canada, but provisions of the *Indian Act*, the *Historic Sites and Monuments Act*, and the *National Parks Act* can be used to stop undesirable or unauthorized excavations on land under federal jurisdiction.

Under the *Indian Act* it is illegal to trespass on a reserve or to remove any property from a reserve without the written consent of the Minister of Indian and Northern Affairs. The *Historic Sites and Monuments Act* gives the Minister the authority to make agreements to purchase land for the purpose of preserving any historic place. The *National Parks Act* prohibits the removal of any property from a National Park without the written permission of the Superintendent.

Provincial Laws

ALBERTA

The *Alberta Heritage Act* of 1973, amended in 1974 and in 1975 amended and renamed the *Alberta Historical Resources Act*, requires any person pursuing archaeological excavation or field surveys on any lands in Alberta to hold a valid permit issued by the Minister of Culture. Permits are normally issued only to applicants holding a Masters degree in archaeology or an equivalent combination of academic training and field experience. An application may be granted to applicants who do not meet this requirement, however, if they are working under

the supervision of a qualified professional archaeologist.

The 1975 amendments to the Act increase the punitive provisions for contravening the Act from $5,000 and six months imprisonment to $50,000 and twelve months imprisonment. For further information on the provisions of the *Alberta Historical Resources Act* and 'the guidelines of qualifications to undertake excavation or surveys, contact the Archaeological Survey of Alberta, 10158 103 Street, Edmonton, Alberta.

BRITISH COLUMBIA

The *Archaeological and Historic Sites Protection Act* of 1972 gives the Provincial Secretary the right to designate a site or parcel of land as an "archaeological site" and therefore under the protection of the Act. Likewise, land threatened by the construction of dams, railroads, pipe lines, or the extraction of natural resources, or other industrial activity are under the protection of the Act. Under provisions of section 7 the Provincial Secretary may require the person or agency responsible for such development to provide sufficient funds for adequate archaeological investigation and he may ask that development activity be suspended while archaeological excavations are being carried out. The Act also prohibits the destruction, desecration or removal of a burial place, Indian painting or rock-carving or Indian habitation site or other site on Crown lands except in the manner authorized by the permit, even in cases where a site has not been officially designated.

Permits are required to excavate or alter a site under the jurisdiction of the law, or to remove, move, or alter any object from such a site. Such permits are valid for the year in which they are issued, and submission of complete excavation and site survey reports are required before the end of the calendar year.

Further information on the Act may be obtained from the Provincial Archaeologist, The Archaeological Sites Advisory Board of British Columbia, Box 200, Parliament Buildings, Victoria, B.C.

MANITOBA

The *Historic Sites and Objects Act* requires anyone planning an excavation in the province to obtain a permit for the work. The holder of a permit must comply with all conditions prescribed by the regulations of the Act, including the keeping of records, photographs and drawings of the results of the excavation.

Ownership of any artifact found in an excavation is vested in the owner of the land in which the artifact is found, except skeletal remains, title of which is vested in the Government. Under section 13(3) no one is allowed to take any artifact from the province without a valid permit issued under the regulations.

For further information about archaeological work in Manitoba write to the Historic Resources Branch, Department of Tourism, Recreation and Cultural Affairs, 200 Vaughan Street, Winnipeg, Manitoba.

NEW BRUNSWICK

The *Historic Sites Protection Act* of 1954 as amended in 1958 and 1961, requires that any person excavating an historic site in New Brunswick must hold a permit issued by the Minister of Education. The Minister may designate any site to be of historical interest and therefore subject to this Act.

Under section 4(1) of the Act, before an application is made to the Minister, a prospective applicant must publish in two consecutive issues of the *Royal Gazette* a notice stating that application for a permit is going to be made to the Minister. The notice must specify the name and address of the applicant, the nature of the work proposed, and the location of the historic site.

The Minister of Education may stipulate such terms and conditions for archaeological work as he may deem advisable. All historical objects under the Act or in contravention of the Act must be deposited in the New Brunswick Museum or another institution so designated by the Minister.

All permit holders are required to have the consent of the landowner before beginning an excavation and are liable to compensate the landowner for any damage to the property resulting from excavation.

At the end of each season's field work or upon expiration of a permit, the permit holder must furnish the Minister with a full report of the work done and the information obtained from the excavation. The Minister of Education can revoke a permit at any time.

For further information about archaeological work in New Brunswick write to the Historical Resources Administration, Box 6000, Fredericton, New Brunswick.

NEWFOUNDLAND AND LABRADOR

The *Historic Objects, Sites and Records Act* of 1973 as amended, requires every person pursuing archaeological investigation in the province, including studies, surveys and examinations, to obtain a permit issued by the Minister of Tourism. One of the conditions of a permit stipulates that all artifactual material is the property of the Government of Newfoundland and Labrador and the Newfoundland Museum is the designated repository for all artifacts recovered in an excavation. Further information on archaeological work in Newfoundland and Labrador can be obtained from the Historic Resources Division, Department of Tourism, Confederation Building, St. John's, Newfoundland.

NOVA SCOTIA

There are no laws directly regulating archaeological excavation in the province, but under certain situations the *Treasure Trove Act* and the *Provincial Parks Act* of 1959 can be invoked to stop any undesirable archaeological work.

The *Treasure Trove Act* gives the Provincial Secretary the right to license the search for treasure (defined as precious stones or metal in a state other than their natural state). Under the *Provincial Parks Act* the Minister of Lands and Forests is able to purchase, expropriate, or otherwise acquire land for a park, including areas of historical interest, and thereby control the excavation of any site within the park's boundaries.

For further details on archaeological work in Nova Scotia contact the Minister of Lands and Forests, or the Provincial Secretary, where an excavation is likely to come under their particular jurisdiction. The Director of the Nova Scotia Museum, 1747 Summer Street, Halifax, should be contacted regarding archaeological work in the province.

ONTARIO

The *Ontario Heritage Act* of 1974 gives the Minister of Culture and Recreation the power to license all archaeological exploration, archaeological survey, and field work in Ontario. The Minister is also responsible for the designation of properties of historic and archaeological significance. The Minister may determine the conditions under which any archaeological work is to be conducted.

At the close of each season's field work every licensee is required to file with the Minister a report containing full details of the work done, including details of any stratification or other chronological evidence. The report must also include information on the precise location of the site and a statement of the methods used to perform excavation or survey work and to record data. A detailed plan complete with representative photographs and sectional drawings, a description of the cultural content of the site, a catalogue of all materials recovered and a preliminary interpretation resulting from a summary examination of these finds, are to be included. Finally, a statement of the professional and material means available to ensure the continuity of the research, and a statement of the restorative and protective means taken at the site should be included in the report.

Under section 66(1) of the *Act*, the Minister of Culture and Recreation may direct that any object taken under the authority of a license or a permit be deposited in a public institution that he may designate.

For further details on the Ontario Heritage Act and the regulations under the Act, write to the Heritage Administration Branch, Minister of Culture and Recreation, Queen's Park, Toronto.

PRINCE EDWARD ISLAND

The *Archaeological Investigation Act* of 1970 requires every person or organization planning an excavation to first obtain a license from the Provincial Archivist. The archivist has the right to supervise and inspect any excavation, and to revoke a license at any time. Permits are not required for studies or surveys which do not involve alteration or removal from the soil of any historic object. For further information about excavation in the province, write to the Provincial Archivist, Public Archives, Box 1000, Charlottetown, P.E.I.

QUEBEC

The *Cultural Property Act* of 1972 and the regulations of June 1973 respecting archaeological research strictly control archaeological work in the province. No person may undertake excavations or surveys to find archaeological property or sites without having an archaeological research permit from the Minister of Cultural Affairs. A permit may be issued for excavation or field survey by the Minister upon the recommendation of a committee composed of three archaeologists. This permit is good for one year from the date of issue.

An applicant for a permit must include the written consent of the owner of the property, and a record of the professional qualifications of the applicant and each person taking part in a dig. Accompanying the application for a permit must be a statement of the archaeological research programme including the nature of the research, the methods of dating, recording and cataloguing of documents, the methods of conservation and restoration of objects and architectural remains. Under the law the government may study an application for up to two months before announcing whether or not it has been approved. Each permit holder is required to submit to the Minister an annual report stating the work carried out, the description of findings, a copy of notes, plans, and drawings, as well as the catalogue of documents and photographs, and a statement of means available to ensure the continuity of research and its successful conclusion. Further information on the Act and an application for an archaeological research permit may be obtained from the Service d'Archéologie et d'Ethnologie, Ministère des Affaires Culturelles, Gouvernement du Québec, 6, rue Université, Québec, G1R 4R7.

SASKATCHEWAN

There are two laws by which archaeological activity in Saskatchewan can be regulated. Under the provisions of the *Provincial Parks, Protected Areas, Recreation Sites and Antiquities Act* of 1960 any area of the province can be declared a "protected area" and when so designated, is under the control of the Department of Tourism and Renewable Resources.

No one may excavate at or explore a provincial park or protected area without a permit from the Minister. The Minister has the right to prescribe the manner and extent of an archaeological excavation in a provincial park or protected area, and can stipulate any other terms or conditions for archaeological work.

Artifacts obtained in contravention to the Act may be declared the property of the Crown and subject to disposal at the discretion of the Minister. It is illegal to buy, sell, trade or otherwise dispose of any archaeological object that has been taken from any part of Saskatchewan without giving the Minister an opportunity to acquire the object at its market value.

The *Saskatchewan Heritage Act* of 1975 gives the Minister the authority to designate any property of interest for among other assets, its archaeological interest, as a "protected property".

A permit is required for archaeological excavations on any protected property. Regulations which delineate the form and scope of permits are being formulated and will be available from the Minister of Tourism and Renewable Resources, Administration Building, Regina, Saskatchewan.

YUKON AND NORTHWEST TERRITORIES

Under the *Yukon Archaeological Sites Regulations* no one can excavate or investigate any archaeological site in the Yukon without a permit from the Minister of Indian and Northern Affairs, Ottawa. The regulations require every permit holder to furnish in duplicate the details of stratification, a descriptive catalogue of all specimens collected, and a copy of all photographs taken and all maps and plans made in connection with the work, and such other information as the Minister may require.

All artifacts from excavations must be submitted to the Minister to be deposited at such places as the Minister may designate.

The *Northwest Territories Archaeological Sites Regulations* are similar in most details to those of the Yukon. Further details on archaeological work in the Northwest Territories can also be obtained from the Minister of Indian and Northern Affairs, Ottawa.

Bibliography

The following list of material for further reading includes books treating various aspects of field archaeology in Canada and elsewhere. Additional references are given in the text in conjunction with specific topics.

GENERAL BOOKS ON FIELD ARCHAEOLOGY

Alexander, John, *The Directing of Archaeological Excavations*. London: John Baker, 1970.

Buchanan, R.A., ed., *The Theory and Practice of Industrial Archaeology*. Bath: Bath University Press, 1968.

Coles, John, *Field Archaeology In Britain*. London: Methuen & Co., 1972.

Crawford, O.S.G., *Archaeology in the Field*. London: Phoenix House, Ltd., 1953.

Hole, Frank and Heizer, Robert F., *An Introduction to Prehistoric Archaeology*. 3rd ed. New York: Holt, Rinehart & Winston, 1973.

Hudson, Kenneth, *Handbook for Industrial Archaeologists*. London: John Baker, 1967.

Hume, Ivor Noël, *Historical Archaeology*. New York: Alfred Knopf, 1972.

Kenyon, K.M., *Beginning In Archaeology*. London: J.M. Dent & Co., 1964.

Pannell, J.P.M., *The Techniques of Industrial Archaeology*. Edited by J. Kenneth Major. Newton Abbot: David & Charles, 1974.

Piggott, Stuart, *Approach to Archaeology*. London: A. & C. Black, 1959.

Pyddoke, E., *What Is Archaeology?* London: John Baker, 1964.

Webster, Graham, *Practical Archaeology*. 2nd ed. London: A. & C. Black, 1974.

Wheeler, (Sir) R.E.M., *Archaeology From the Earth*. London: Penguin Books, 1956.

THE FIELD SURVEY

Aston, Michael, and Rowley, T., *Landscape Archaeology*. Newton Abbot: David & Charles, 1974.

Atkinson, R.J.C., "Resistivity Surveying in Archaeology." In *The Scientist and Archaeology*, edited by Edward Pyddoke, pp. 1-30. London: Phoenix House Ltd., 1963.

Fowler, E., ed., *Field Surveying In British Archaeology*. London: Council for British Archaeology, 1972.

Hoskins, W.G., *Fieldwork In Local History.* London: Faber & Faber, 1967.

MAPS AND AERIAL PHOTOGRAPHS

Ministry of Defense, *Manual of Map Reading.* London: H.M.S.O., 1973.

St. Joseph, J.K., ed., *The Uses of Air Photography.* London: John Baker Publications Ltd., 1966.

Sebert, L.M., *Every Square Inch.* Ottawa: Department of Energy, Mines and Resources, 1970.

ESTABLISHING A GRID

Fryer, D.H., *Surveying for Archaeologists.* 4th ed. Durham: University of Durham, 1971.

Pryor, Francis, *Earthmoving on Open Archaeological Sites.* Edited by J.P. Wild. Peterborough, England: Nene Valley Research Committee, 1974.

Ripa, Louis C., *Surveying Manual.* New York: McGraw-Hill Book Co., 1964.

Royer, King, *Applied Field Surveying.* New York: John Wiley & Sons Ltd., 1958.

Vose, James, *Dumpy Level Work.* London: Cleaver-Hume Ltd., 1956.

SOILS AND SOIL LAYERS

Canada Department of Agriculture, *The System of Soil Classification for Canada.* Rev. ed. Ottawa: Information Canada, 1974.

Cornwall, I.W., *Soils for the Archaeologist.* London: Phoenix House, Ltd., 1958.

Cornwall, I.W., "Soil Science Helps the Archaeologist." In *The Scientist and Archaeology,* edited by Edward Pyddoke. London: Phoenix House Ltd., 1961.

Kolinke, Helmut, *Soil Physics.* New York: McGraw-Hill, Inc., 1968.

Pyddoke, Edward, *Stratification for the Archaeologist.* London: Phoenix House, 1961.

Soil Survey Staff, *Soil Survey Manual.* Washington, D.C.: U.S. Department of Agriculture, 1951.

ARCHAEOLOGICAL PHOTOGRAPHY

Bracegirdle, Brian, *Photography for Books and Reports.* Newton Abbot: David & Charles, 1970.

Conlon, V.M., *Camera Techniques in Archaeology.* London: John Baker, 1973.

Cookson, M.B., *Photography for Archaeologists.* London: Max Parrish, 1954.

Matthews, S.K., *Photography in Archaeology & Art.* London: John Baker, 1968.

Simmons, Harold C., *Archaeological Photography.* London: University of London Press, 1969.

South, Stanley A., "Photography in Historical Archaeology," *Historical Archaeology* II (1968): 73-113.

FIELD CONSERVATION AND SAMPLING

Council for British Archaeology, *Handbook of Scientific Aids and Evidence for Archaeologists.* London: Council for British Archaeology, 1970.

Dimbleby, Geoffrey, *Plants and Archaeology.* London: John Baker, 1967.

Dowman, Elizabeth A., *Conservation in Field Archaeology.* London: Methuen & Co., 1970.

Leigh, David, comp., *First Aid for Finds.* Southampton, Eng: Rescue, 1972.

Plenderleith, H.J., and Werner, A.E., *The Conservation of Antiquities and Works of Art.* 2nd ed. London: Oxford University Press, 1971.

Werner, A.E., *The Conservation of Cultural Property.* Paris: Unesco, 1968.

PREPARING THE EXCAVATION REPORT

Brodribb, Conant, *Drawing Archaeological Finds for Publication.* London: John Baker, 1970.

Collison, Robert L., *Indexes & Indexing.* London: Ernest Benn Ltd., 1972.

Geological Survey of Canada, *Guide to Authors.* Rev. ed. Ottawa: Information Canada, 1975.

Grinsell, Leslie; Rhatz, Philip; and Price-Williams, David, *The Preparation of Archaeological Reports.* 2nd ed. London: John Baker, 1974.

Hart's Rules for Compositors and Readers. 37th ed. London: Oxford University Press, 1970.

Hodgkiss, A.G., *Maps for Books and Theses.* Newton Abbot: David & Charles, 1972.

Modern Language Association, *MLA Style Sheet.* 2nd ed. New York: Modern Language Association of America, 1951.

University of Chicago, *A Manual of Style.* 12th ed. Chicago: The University of Chicago Press, 1974.

INDEX